The King Ranch Story

Truth and Myth

A history of the oldest and greatest ranch in Texas

Mona D. Sizer

Republic of Texas Press

Library of Congress Cataloging-in-Publication Data

Sizer, Mona D.
The King Ranch story: Truth and myth: A history of the oldest and greatest ranch in Texas / Mona D. Sizer.
p. cm.
Includes bibliographical references and index.
ISBN 1-55622-680-2
1. King Ranch (Tex.)—History. 2. King Ranch (Tex.)—Biography. I. Title.
F392.K47S59 1999
976.4'472—dc21 98-51944
CIP

Republic of Texas Press is an imprint of Wordware Publishing, Inc.

Printed in the United States of America

ISBN 1-55622-680-2
10 9 8 7 6 5 4 3 2 1
9902

All inquiries for volume purchases of this book should be addressed to Wordware Publishing, Inc., at 2320 Los Rios Boulevard, Plano, Texas 75074. Telephone inquiries may be made by calling:

(972) 423-0090

Contents

Part IV
A Bloody Peace

The Truth

The Myth

Part V
"As I Myself Might Do"

The Truth

The Myth

Part VI
"The Walled Kingdom of Texas"

Acknowledgements

I would like to acknowledge, first and above all, W. C. Jameson, writer, teacher, taleteller, singer, historian, and my very good friend, who told me about Republic of Texas Press and recommended me to them.

I would like to acknowledge Ginnie Siena Bivona, who sought me out and gave me the opportunity to write this book and to turn my career in another direction. Her encouragement and enthusiasm for the project carried me along much faster than I would have thought possible.

I would like to thank my husband, James Sizer, who has always been my support through all my endeavors and who took so many of the wonderful pictures that will give the reader a sense of the rolling vistas and calm majesty that is the King Ranch today.

Thanks also to a guide named Dusty, who drove us around the ranch and told us so much of the story. Thanks to the co-operative and knowledgeable people at the King Ranch Archives—Lisa A. Neely and Jamene Toelkes. Thanks to all the *Kineños* with whom Jim and I came in contact, who were so proud and happy to tell us about the place where they live and work.

Thanks to all my history teachers and English teachers who taught me to love history and literature and to do the research necessary to write this book. In every sense this book can be said to be the work of many hands.

KING

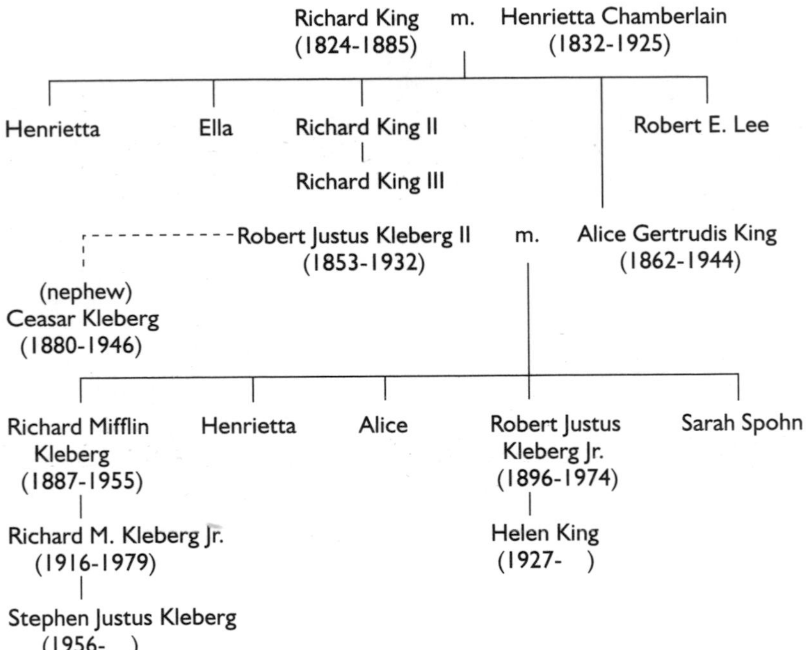
Richard King m. Henrietta Chamberlain
(1824-1885) (1832-1925)
Henrietta
Ella
Richard King II
Richard King III
Robert E. Lee
Robert Justus Kleberg II m. Alice Gertrudis King
(1853-1932) (1862-1944)
(nephew)
Ceasar Kleberg
(1880-1946)
Richard Mifflin Kleberg
(1887-1955)
Richard M. Kleberg Jr.
(1916-1979)
Stephen Justus Kleberg
(1956-)
Henrietta
Alice
Robert Justus Kleberg Jr.
(1896-1974)
Helen King
(1927-)
Sarah Spohn

Part I

Sailor on Horseback

Captain Richard King
(Courtesy of the Texas and Southwestern
Cattle Raisers Foundation, Fort Worth, Texas.)

The Truth

The Land Nobody Wanted

The Texas cowboy calls it the brush country or the chaparral. The Texas *vaquero* speaks of the *brasada* or the *monte*. The Anglo-Americans who came to Texas in the early 1800s called it Wild Horse Desert. To the Texas Rangers, who had to bring the law to it, it was the Nueces Strip.

History and legend name it *El Desierto de los Muertos*, the Desert of the Dead.

With reason.

The Coahuiltecans were the first Indians known to have lived there. In order to survive its harsh conditions, they had to evolve a culture unique in Texas history and almost unique in North America. They became simple gatherers who grubbed for their food—spiders, ant eggs, lizards, rattlesnakes, worms, insects, and rotting wood. If they caught a fish in the brackish water of the lagoons, they set it in the sun for several days to collect flies to breed maggots. When it was crawling and stinking, they ate the enriched food with gusto.

When the water was too brackish or water holes dried up entirely, they sucked liquid from the prickly pear.

They ground flour out of agave bulbs and maguey, sotol and lechuguilla. Only *maguey*, the word for century plant, appears in ordinary Spanish dictionaries. It refers to the spiny leaves of the plant.

More specialized dictionaries list the others. *Agave* was another word for century plant referring to the entire plant. In this case, the bulb would have been gathered before the plant could bloom and die. *Lechuguilla* was simply another cactus.

Fermented drinks were very popular probably because most of the water sources were brackish. *Sotol* is variously yucca and Spanish dagger. The Coahuiltecans fermented it and made a kind of *pulque*, much like what is still drunk in Mexico today.

They also made a drink fermented from red laurel beans. For purposes we can only suspect, they made a mildly hallucinatory tea from peyote cactus.

Out of the dung of deer and out of their own feces, they picked seeds, then roasted and chewed them. These they referred to as the Second Harvest.

The Coahuiltecans moved about the semiarid land in small familial bands. The climate was hot and dry from March through November. The other three months were cold and wet only for short periods of time. They developed no effective weapons nor protective cover. No large predatory animals lived in *El Desierto de los Muertos*. No other peoples threatened them because no one else wanted the land they moved through.

They practiced infanticide, killing girl-children because they believed their land was already overpopulated. What they killed, they had no compunction about eating.

Nevertheless, with good reason they feared the people from the northern curve of the Gulf Coast. The Karankawas, the eaters of men, were famous for their savagery and bestiality. Naked, because they had no means of acquiring nor making clothing, they coated themselves with mud and foul-smelling fish oil as a barrier against the prevailing winds off the Gulf and the swarms of disease-bearing mosquitos. Legendary cannibals, they were supposed to have captured little children and eaten them as they moved nomadically about the coastal plain.

The Spaniards gave the Karankawas a wide berth. The padres built two missions along the coast but quickly moved them inland when the warlike Karankawas attacked.

Likewise, they built no missions in *El Desierto de los Muertos*. The semidesert was too arid and inhospitable. Though they fed the Coahuiltecans who wandered northward toward San Antonio, when they tried to teach them Christianity, the simple people couldn't grasp the concepts. When the churchmen wanted to put them to work, the Indians quickly drifted away.

The holy men did not pursue them with any vigor. They were interested in Christianizing Indians with at most a moderate level of barbarism.

So the Coahuiltecans continued their primitive ways until the beginning of the nineteenth century when Anglo-American expansion into Texas drove the Karankawas south into the semidesert. There the bigger, fiercer peoples struck terror among the unarmed, unorganized groups of gatherers whom they killed or drove south of the Rio Grande.

The Karankawas' cannibalism is disputed today, since none of the Spanish explorers actually witnessed them at such a meal and lived to tell about it. However, given the semidesert conditions and the lack of large game animals to support true hunting, the chances are good that they, like the "peaceful" Coahuiltecans, ate what they could find.

Even the great buffalo herds didn't venture south of the Balcones Escarpment. The heat was too intense for their shaggy bodies covered in curly brown fur. The land was too dry for a herd to find enough water to drink, much less to wallow in.

But even the land nobody wanted could be put to use by desperate men. In the Bourbon kingdom of Spain, in 1805, a desperate man ruled. King Carlos IV needed as many supporters as he could rally for his feeble monarchy. More to the point, he was alarmed by the rumblings of revolt from his subjects in Mexico as well as those in the rest of Central and South America. Hoping for the support of the wealthy Spanish-Mexican *rancheros*, he gave away many leagues of land where the Karankawas roamed.

His grants were crackling rolls of parchment written in elegant script, stamped and over-stamped with the imperial crowns and the castles and lions of Castile and Aragon. What did they really delineate? One survey names landmarks such as "*La Laguna Escondida*," translated as The Lost Lagoon, and "The Boundary called *El Lobo*," The Wolf. Did anyone actually know where those landmarks lay? Did anyone care?

The men to whom one of these grants was given in 1806 lived safe and prosperous on the southern side of the Rio Grande. Don José Lorenzo de la Garza and his two sons José Domingo and José Julian lived in Camargo on the southern side of the river they called the Rio Bravo.

In 1808 they actually tried to take possession of their new property, 53,000 acres of the *brasada* that comprised the grant named *De la Garza Santa Gertrudis*. They built houses and corrals. They moved herds northward and put herdsman on the range to work.

In 1814 Don José Lorenzo was killed while shaking hands with the Indians. Thereafter, his sons made no effort even to ride over the lands. The buildings were abandoned. The herds were driven back to Mexico or allowed to escape. Let the Karankawas keep their Desert of the Dead. To the landowners' eyes it was worthless as perhaps King Carlos himself was. His gift was a token only.

To members of a civilized society, the land was untenable. It would probably have remained as it was except that it was still overrun with tough animals from the semi-deserts of Africa and Spain. The first cattle, whose great long horns looked much like those of the cattle in Egyptian tomb paintings, came with Columbus in 1493. The first horses, Barbs from Morocco and Andalusians from southern Spain, came with Cortéz.

From those few and countless others imported as the Spanish came in fleets to find Aztec and Inca gold, great herds evolved. The animals adapted easily to the land so like their own. *Rancheros* bred their own herds all across Mexico. When some strayed, were lost, or were stolen, the toughest stallions collected their own bands of mares. The strongest bulls sired the most calves. Across the Rio Bravo they swam. The Desert of the Dead was life to them. Unchecked by natural predators, they roamed the land nobody wanted during the two-decades-long war for Mexican independence from Spain.

In 1834 a grant for the *Rincón de Santa Gertrudis* was issued for Juan Mendiola, also of Camargo, but he never took possession of his "hidden valley" of 15,500 acres. By that time a new group, the Texans, were ranging over Wild Horse Desert. They were determined to gain independence from Mexico.

After Texas declared itself a republic on March 2, 1836, four days before the Alamo fell, Thomas Jefferson Rusk, its first secretary of war, realized Texas could not feed its volunteer troops. He detailed men to rustle herds of Mexican beeves south of the Nueces.

So began the legend of the *cowboys*. For months thereafter bands of ten to fifteen horsemen, young and wild, armed with Bowie knives and muzzle-loaders, would cross the river to rustle as many as two hundred head of cattle at a time. Since the longhorns were half wild and dangerous, they didn't herd well.

The cowboys would cut the throat of the herd bull and bunch the rest. Then they would set the herd to running. They would swing their slickers and lariats and yell like banshees. For as long as twenty-four hours, or until the cattle were exhausted and all pursuit abandoned, they would stampede the leaderless cattle through the brush and back across the river.

Their destination was the loading pens at Goliad, seventy-five miles north of the Nueces, where anti-Mexican emotions ran highest. There Colonel Fannin and over four hundred soldiers had surrendered. On March 27, 1836, they were marched out and shot down by Mexican troops acting under orders from the Mexican dictator General Antonio Lopez de Santa Anna.

On April 21, 1836, the Texans won their independence. General Sam Houston secured it by capturing the general at San Jacinto. The Republic of Texas was born.

The cowboys, however, did not stop their raids because Mexico did not recognize her upstart neighbor to the north. She was determined not to give up one square foot of land easily. For nine years the southern boundary of the new republic was disputed.

The Mexicans declared it to be the Nueces River north of *El Desierto de los Muertos* that the Texans commonly called Wild Horse Desert. The Texans claimed the boundary was the Rio Grande, which Mexico called Rio Bravo.

Between the Rio Grande and the Nueces lay one hundred forty miles of seacoast bordering more than two hundred miles of semidesert. These were thousands of square miles that no one cared about, except as a matter of principle.

For most of the nineteenth century, sorties of *los diablos Tejanos* or Texians or Texans attacked or were attacked by Mexicans whenever they stumbled across each other. The desert was uninhabited except by the hated and feared Cronks (the Karankawas), who added their savage ambushes to the murderous mix.

Only south of the Rio Grande at Camargo, Reynosa, and Matamoros, and in Brownsville on the north, settlements were growing. People thrived in the delta of the big river just as they do today.

How much longer the land would have been disputed can only be guessed. Perhaps no one would have cared to press the matter had not President John Tyler of the United States annexed the Republic of Texas in 1845.

The young Republic claimed all the land north and east of the Rio Grande not already included in the Louisiana Purchase. This included much of present New Mexico and part of Colorado. It further implied that the land west of the river—the remainder of New Mexico, Arizona, and California should also belong to the United States.

The Mexican government was outraged.

Political wits of the time noted ironically that, "Tyler got the glory, while Polk got the war that made Taylor president."

In 1845 General Zachary Taylor, "Old Rough and Ready," in his palmetto hat and plain blue frock coat without brass buttons, landed at Corpus Christi at the mouth of the Nueces. The cry from Washington was "Manifest Destiny." It was the duty of Congress to settle the West. Many legislators made speeches stating that the United States should rule all of the North American continent. Talk ran high that Mexico, herself in a state of political turmoil, should be annexed.

By order of President Polk, in January 1846 Taylor advanced his troops, all 2,288 of them, to what was to become the undisputed boundary of the United States—the Rio Grande. Though outnumbered, he committed his men to battles at Palo Alto and Resaca de la Palma. Victorious at both, eventually, he crossed the Rio Grande and won at Buena Vista outside Monterrey.

To hold the delta and occupy northern Mexico, Taylor needed supplies. Riverboats were commissioned to carry material from the supply depot at *El Paso de los Brazos de Santiago*, translated as The Pass of the Arms of Saint James. They were paddle wheelers suitable to hug the coast for ten miles to *La Boca del Rio*, The Mouth of the River, then sail up the Rio Grande to Camargo. There their cargos and reinforcements could be transported overland to Monterrey, where General Taylor was preparing to do battle to capture the city.

One of the many men to answer Taylor's call for the flotilla was Captain Mifflin Kenedy. A Pennsylvania Quaker with a head for making money, he had migrated from Florida, sized up the situation, and promptly sent for the ambitious, young friend who later became his partner.

Twenty-three-year-old Richard King received his first orders from the U.S. Army Quartermaster's office in Brownsville, Texas, June 13, 1847. He reported for duty as one of three second pilots on the recently commissioned sternwheeler *Colonel Cross*.

He served just seventeen days before he was transferred to act as first pilot on the *Corvette*, another sternwheeler. The willingness to dare, to put himself in harm's way, brought him there. Later he was transferred back to the

Colonel Cross as its captain. Shortly afterward he celebrated his twenty-fourth birthday.

In November 1847, eight months after the battle of Buena Vista that had secured all of northern Mexico for America, the *Colonel Cross* carried General Zachary Taylor back downriver from Carmargo to his own manifest destiny—the White House.

In February 1848, by the Treaty of Guadalupe Hidalgo, the United States of America paid Mexico $15,000,000 and assumed Americans' claims of another $3,250,000 in exchange for the states of California, Nevada, Utah, Arizona, parts of New Mexico, Colorado, and Wyoming.

Manifest Destiny became "from sea to shining sea."

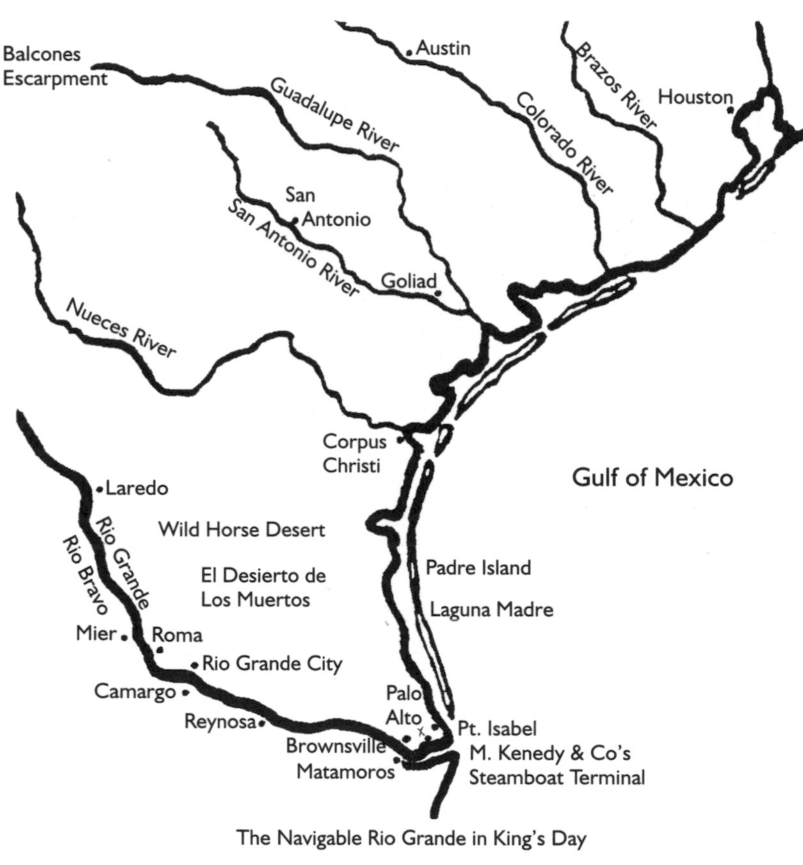

The Navigable Rio Grande in King's Day

Miles by Steamboat: 253	
Gulf of Mexico to Brownsville	50
Brownsville to Reynosa	128
Reynosa to Rio Grande City	42
Rio Grande City to Roma	20
Roma to Mier	13

The Riverman

Unfortunately for Richard King, the steamboats on the Rio Grande were no longer needed. Decommissioned, the *Colonel Cross* rotted for a year at Brazos de Santiago while its young captain ran a flophouse and grogshop where he was the proprietor, bedmaker, bartender, and bouncer. Leading this unsavory life, he bided his time until the treaty was signed. At that time the U.S. Quartermaster put the flotilla up for sale.

For $750 King bought the *Colonel Cross*, a ship for which the government had paid $14,000. He was back in business hauling goods out of rich central Mexico down the Rio Grande to the Gulf of Mexico. As captain of his own ship, he became part of the Manifest Destiny of the newest area of the United States of America.

Operating a single vessel as owner-master-pilot had advantages. King did all that work himself. He could read and write. He had taught himself to cast accounts. He kept his own books and answered to nobody. He cut his payroll to a cook, an engineer whom he assisted when the need arose, and more than a dozen Mexican stokers and deckhands, among them a giant of a man, young and strong and looking for a *jefe* to attach himself to. His name was

Faustino Villa, and he remained at King's side all of the captain's life.

King had enough business to operate the boat twenty-four hours a day. A typical voyage would require him to pick up cargo at Camargo—pig lead, hides, mules, salt, bones and tallow, bales and sacks of wool. Loaded with raw materials, he sailed down to Boca del Rio where he transferred the cargo onto Gulf steamers.

There he picked up manufactured goods—mining machinery, tools, wagons, harnesses, dry goods, tobacco, wines and liquors, rough-sawed lumber, bales of cotton—everything and anything necessary to rebuild war ravaged Mexico.

At the end of the return trip, his partner Mifflin Kenedy carried the goods by mule train into the interior and returned with saddlebags full of Mexican silver profits. The peso—legal tender in Texas until 1857—was of a higher grade of silver than its equivalent American dollar. Kenedy sold it as bullion and made yet another profit.

But King wasn't getting rich. The *Colonel Cross* was too slow, too small, too light, and required too much money for repairs. The same was true of the other boats operating on the Rio Grande. King was getting discouraged.

Then Kenedy saw an opportunity to go into business with Charles Stillman, a prominent merchant and trader, of Matamoros. He suggested to King that all three men go into the shipping business together.

King was tired of the old decommissioned riverboat. He had discovered through bitter experiences that it hadn't been well built in the beginning. Moreover, it was unsuitable for the river it was expected to navigate on. Its draft was too deep for the mud skimming the Rio Grande required in too many places along its looping, twisting length.

Half the old boats that had been decommissioned a year before were already out of business. The *Colonel Cross* was bound in that direction sooner than later. King was tired of working twenty-four hours, seven days a week. He was ready to go to California where gold had been discovered.

His partners knew he was too valuable to lose. Mifflin Kenedy talked to him. Charles Stillman, the eighteen-year-old son of wealthy Connecticut Yankee Francis Stillman, who had purchased many of the remainder of the decommissioned vessels, talked to him. James O'Donnell, the captain in charge of the remaining vessels, talked to him.

Still King saw many problems. He argued that they ought to sink all the boats and start over again with two different fleets—one for the Gulf and one for the Rio Grande. They ought to build warehouses for their goods. They ought to build docks to load properly. They ought to build a terminal to handle business transactions as well as passengers.

He drew them diagrams of the two different kinds of ships they needed. Stillman put up the money. Mifflin Kenedy left for Pittsburgh by way of New Orleans to commission the ships to be built according to King's recommendations.

Still, Richard King was casting restless eyes toward California, until one seemingly ordinary day in February 1850.

~ ~ ~

The Rio Grande delta is hot three hundred sixty days a year. The other five days the temperature may drop below freezing for a few hours. Usually during the winter months, a blue norther whistles in, dropping the temperature to forty degrees Fahrenheit. Everyone throws an extra quilt on the bed and dresses in the cold the next morning.

By noon, the Gulf breezes have collided with the cold front and driven it back where it came from or warmed it until it is merely a breath of coolness beneath an overcast sky. The sun comes out and everything warm becomes hot.

The river was mud-brown and low. The Rocky Mountain snows hadn't melted yet and filled it to the banks. Undoubtedly it stank of the refuse dumped into it by all the villages and towns for miles along its length.

On such a day, Captain King gave a hard left rudder and steered the *Colonel Cross* around the last bend toward the Brownsville riverfront. At the slip where he usually moored, one of the old U.S. Quartermaster boats had taken his spot. It was the *Whiteville,* a boat old when the navy had commissioned her.

Not only was it moored at what he considered to be his slip, it was blocking his way.

He blew his whistle again and again. Nothing happened. Nothing moved.

Out of the wheelhouse he shot, turning the air blue with his curses. He bellowed at the anchored vessel calling her a filthy, rat-infested tub. To the dockhands watching open-mouthed, he yelled that she ought to be hauled out into the middle of the Gulf and sunk or sold for the scrap lumber and equipment she carried.

He demanded to know who had the gall to tie "that goddamn tub" there in the way anyhow?

Faustino Villa tried to warn him. While King was upriver, the *Whiteville* had been bought for a houseboat and rented to the Presbyterian preacher. The Reverend Hiram Chamberlain had come from Tennessee to establish the very first Protestant church on all the length of the Rio Grande.

The information only made King more irate. He cleared his throat to let fly with his opinions of preachers and churches.

Then a door opened. A young lady stepped out of the *Whiteville's* cabin.

Across the curling brown water in the bright sunlight, they saw each other for the first time. Miss Henrietta Maria Morse Chamberlain, the minister's seventeen-year-old-daughter, and Captain Richard King, the twenty-five-year-old self-made, self-taught orphan from the streets of New York.

The family stories don't tell what she was wearing that afternoon. It was probably a simple cotton or wool dress, high necked and long-sleeved with lace or ruching at the throat and wrists. Beneath the tight-fitting waist the full skirt would have belled out over modest crinolines. She might have worn a small hoop.

Because she was still a maiden lady, her long hair might have been caught back with side combs or tied with a ribbon so it hung down her back. Since she never would have cut it, it probably hung almost to her waist. She would have worn no makeup. A modest young lady in those times might have dusted herself lightly with body powder after her bath, but that was the extent of her coverup. She definitely would not have been tanned by the bright Texas sun. No lady would ever allow her delicate white skin to become sallow.

Undoubtedly, she was as different from the women King was used to seeing as day from night.

Undoubtedly, he looked the same to her.

He might have been wearing his billed cap or hat, but he'd probably left his coat in the wheelhouse, or even in his cubbyhole below. Because of the heat of the day, he might have had his shirt sleeves rolled up above his elbows. His pantlegs would have been rolled up too. His feet could have been bare.

Grime from the smokestack probably darkened his face and clothing. He'd sweated until great dark rings stained the material of his shirt beneath his armpits and in the middle of his back. He wouldn't have shaved on his trip. Perhaps he had several days' growth of beard.

His Irish blue eyes, wide with amazement and then with embarrassment, would have stood out like sapphires if she'd been looking at them.

According to the family story, she didn't like what she heard, and she liked what she saw even less. He was filthy and sweaty. His skin was dark as old oak. Moreover, his language was obscene.

To her, he looked like everything she had come with her father to reform and civilize.

To him, she looked like everything he'd ever wanted. Pretty as only a fresh-faced, gently reared girl could be. Outraged, as only a minister's daughter could be.

She looked his boat over. Then in ringing, righteous tones, she told him to look to himself if he wanted to see filthy and rat-infested. She wasn't surprised, she declared. His demeanor and language were examples of everything about him. She tossed her head, turned on her heel with a swish of her skirts, and strode back into the cabin.

He stared after her as if he'd seen his future. All thoughts of California and gold vanished from his mind. He was interested in one thing only. The minister's daughter. And being worthy of her.

But first he had to meet her properly.

To secure an introduction, he turned to his friend Mifflin Kenedy, himself an upright and sober Quaker. If Kenedy couldn't organize a proper meeting—

King couldn't think beyond that point.

Kenedy grinned at his partner, earnest, uncertain, stammering for one of the few occasions in their long friendship.

He could introduce his friend to Miss Chamberlain at a prayer meeting and church social Wednesday evening aboard the *Whiteville*.

In his whole life King had never been to a prayer meeting much less a church social. Back in New York, he'd run away from his apprenticeship when he was eleven years old. He'd signed on as cabin boy on the *Desdemona* bound for Florida and the Gulf waters of Mobile Bay. He'd had only eight months of formal schooling in his entire life. He'd run a flophouse and grogshop. He'd knocked men around with his fists.

He probably ran his hand through his long, unkempt black hair and shook his head.

He was temporarily reprieved from the awful fate of the Presbyterian Church. Before he could work up nerve enough to attend prayer meeting, he and Kenedy happened to come face to face with Miss Chamberlain on the street. Kenedy performed the introductions.

She recognized Richard King immediately as the profane riverboat captain who'd blown his whistle at her. Her brown eyes must have narrowed as she studied him. She was a minister's daughter. Did she recognize a soul to save?

Now that he'd seen her up close, he wanted her more than ever.

Thereafter he attended prayer meetings and attached himself to her whenever he could. The Reverend Hiram Chamberlain wasn't pleased. He had much godlier aspirations than a riverboat captain for his refined Christian daughter.

But she was her father's child. She remembered a letter he'd once written to her while she was away at boarding school and desperately homesick. He told her to quiet her fears and fill her mind and spirit with "noble resolution," to make it the foundation of her life.

With such spirit and mind she regarded Richard King. With noble resolution, she would civilize and Christianize him.

The two ships King had designed arrived, and a Kenedy dock was built at White Ranch at Brazos de Santiago. The big *Grampus* could load cargo there and deliver the cargo to the little *Comanche* for any point upriver on a through bill of lading. Shippers' expenses were cut in half. Soon the other operators on the river found they couldn't compete.

In less than two years, M. Kenedy & Company consisting of Kenedy, King, Stillman, and O'Donnell controlled all water-borne goods in the northern Mexico trade. With a trade monopoly they were making as much as $80,000 a year. Even though they were putting much of their profits into new ships, they were still making a great deal more money than most men in the United States of America before the Civil War.

Their hard-headed business acumen wasn't lost on the Presbyterian minister. Perhaps Kenedy and Stillman were having a good effect on King.

As Henrietta told her family many years later, "In time Reverend Hiram Chamberlain grew to admire the young Captain's sterling upright qualities."

Into the Desert of the Dead

Gideon K. "Legs" Lewis was a Texas war hero. He had carried dispatches for Taylor's troops during the Mexican War. Richard King probably met him in 1851 when Lewis was one of a troop of Texas Rangers camped ten miles from the M. Kenedy & Company wood yard near the White Ranch on the Rio Grande.

They became great friends. Only someone with Lewis's reckless personality could have persuaded the riverboat captain, who rode horseback both poorly and painfully, to put his foot in the stirrup and ride out into the tall grass virtually uninhabited for boundless miles and miles.

From Brownsville at the mouth of Rio Grande in the dry spring of 1852, King and Lewis rode north to see what was being advertised as the first Lone Star Fair in the old Spanish town of Corpus Christi at the mouth of the Nueces.

Alabama trader and huckster Henry Lawrence Kinney had been the only American living south of the Nueces when Texas became a republic in 1836. Naming himself a representative for that part of the state, he became a delegate to the Republic of Texas Convention. For obvious reasons he had insisted that the boundary of Texas had to be the Rio Grande.

Now that his land was part of the United States, he wanted to sell it for nearly a hundred percent profit. To this end he promoted Corpus Christi as "Little Naples" and "The Italy of America."

From him had come the pamphlets Lewis and King had seen. In them he invited one and all to come and buy lots in this soon-to-boom metropolis, this seat of golden opportunity. Not only could they have the chance to buy a piece of paradise, but they would be entertained, educated, enlightened, *et cetera, et cetera* at a Lone Star Fair, the first annual one of its kind.

To see the show and hear the sales talk was one of the reasons King and Lewis rode north into the deserted prairies. The other was the possibility that the prairie might be turned into something more.

Leaving Brownsville, they rode for miles in a shimmer of heat through palmetto thickets and around the edges of *resacas*, whose fingers of brackish water backed up from the Gulf when the tides turned. Still farther along, they dismounted at the Arroyo Colorado. So steep was the bank that they had to lead their horses down into the gully to drink. At that time of the year it had water, but they found it was too salty and unfit for human consumption.

So had Zachary Taylor's troops found it when they marched south from Corpus Christi in 1847. More than two thousand men had marched for more than a hundred miles without finding a single watering hole. On its banks, they dismounted in anticipation only to discover they still had to reach the Rio Grande before they would find water to quench their thirst.

From the *arroyo* Lewis led King over grassy prairie to the deserted *rancho* named *El Sauz*. One look at the crumbling huts and the dry *resaca* told its own story. No one had lived there in a very long time.

Continuing northward they rode through tall dry grass high as their horses' bellies, so high the leather *tapaderos* that protected the fronts of their stirrups left a trail through it. So high it brushed the heels of their boots.

A bank of clouds swept in from the Gulf. The wind freshened and a sudden shower drenched them. Then as suddenly as it came it was gone. Their clothing steamed as the grass steamed. They could smell creosote. Within an hour they were dry.

Here and there the grass seemed choked out by thickets of mesquite, chaparral, and cactus. These were the true *brasada*, brush so thick that to ride a horse through it was impossible. The inch-long thorns would tear an animal to pieces and shred the pants off a man's legs.

Still the prairie was far from deserted. As King and Lewis loped along, living things started up and fled before them. Flocks of wild turkeys darted away. Bevies of quail burst in front of them and whirred off like scatter shot from a twelve gauge. Sidewinders rattled their warnings and slid into the thickets, forked tongues flicking. Overhead an occasional buzzard sailed by, eyes scanning the ground for the weak and dying.

And on the horizon plumes of dust rose where the herds of horses, wild as the deer and the antelope, galloped away with manes and tails streaming.

But no men. The Coahuiltecans, the Karankawas, the Spanish, the Mexicans, the soldiers, even the cowboys. All had left this unrelenting land.

A hundred and twenty-four hard, dry miles they rode until they came to water—a creek called Santa Gertrudis—where King had his first fresh drink since leaving Brownsville.

Forty-five miles still lay between them and Corpus Christi. When they lay down for the night beside clear running water from a strong seep, the grass stood tall around them.

The next day they went on to the Fair. The whole of Nueces County was there, all 698 people. The Methodist church ladies sold cakes and pies. The Catholic church ladies sold embroidered tea napkins. But only about a thousand visitors appeared. Everyone was disappointed—especially Kinney. Despite all the expensive brochures, not more than two thousand visitors came during the duration of the event. He went broke.

But somehow, sometime during those days, Richard King decided that he wanted to buy land. Not the land offered by Kinney, but the land on the bank of the freshwater Santa Gertrudis Creek.

Tha Santa Gertrudis Creek, actually a seep spring, was the first fresh water King found after leaving the Rio Grande. (Author photo)

The way to buy it was not through Lewis, but through the grants from the Mexican owners. The Texas Legislature had confirmed in February 1852 that original Spanish and Mexican land grants were not to be taken over by anyone who simply cared to squat on them. They belonged to the rightful heirs and must be purchased from them if their owners wanted to sell.

Captain King reasoned that he had money for the land, which would probably be cheap since no owners were present. On the other hand, he couldn't build a ranch and stock it only to have his house burned down and his stock run off.

To safeguard his investment and what he vaguely dreamed might be his home, he needed protection. He needed Legs Lewis. Together they planned for the ranger to get himself appointed captain of the Texas Mounted Volunteers. So employed, Legs hired men to patrol and protect the region around Corpus Christi.

ꟺ ꟺ ꟺ

King's cow camp sat on a rise above the creek in the heart of what was once the *Rincón de Santa Gertrudis* grant. It was close to the site Texas Ranger Captain John S. Ford had chosen for his Ranger camp when he'd come through in 1849.

Surveyed by Antonio Canales, Surveyer General of the State of Tamaulipas, on December 21, 1832, the land had been granted to Juan Mendiola of Camargo in 1834. Before he could improve the land, he had died, and it had been abandoned by his family because of the Texas Revolution.

Now King sought out Mendiola's widow and his three sons. None of them was remotely interested in returning to their property. For the sum of three hundred dollars, a windfall for the Mendiolas, he bought title to three and a half leagues of land, 15,500 acres, for less than two cents an acre. When Felix A. Blucher from Corpus Christi went out to make an accurate survey of the Mendiola property, King was one of five chain carriers who assisted in assigning the boundaries for the plat.

To ensure Legs Lewis's participation, King sold a half interest to the young man for two thousand dollars. It was possibly the last time in his life that King sold land, but turning a quick profit was important to him.

Lewis bought a tract of five leagues from Manuel Barrera and another tract of two leagues from Juan Villareal. He sold half interest in those to King for a thousand dollars.

"The Big Santa Gertrudis" was one of the best pieces of ranch land in the region. The Santa Gertrudis Creek ran its entire length, more than twelve miles. From it branched several stream beds that ran water during rainy seasons. It was as big as a medieval fiefdom. The runaway apprentice from the streets of New York had bought more land than the city of New York encompassed.

Still the beginning was inauspicious. In 1852 when Texas Ranger Captain Ford came back through he was unimpressed with King's cow camp. Beside the Santa Gertrudis, he found a collection of mud huts and mesquite corrals. A motley group of *vaqueros*, Texans from Nueces County, and a cowboy or two made up the entire crew. The exact number of men who worked for him in those days is unknown. Probably it changed as men wandered in and out.

In 1854 King and Lewis traced down the single heir to the De La Garza Santa Gertrudis. Praxides Uribe cared so little about his grandfather's land that he did not have perfected documents to prove his ownership.

King was particular in dealing with Uribe. He went to a great deal of effort to discover the original documents to help prove Uribe's claim in order to buy the land from him. All possible title hazards were carefully eliminated. When

Richard King began work on his new *rancho* he wanted no surprises.

ꟺ ꟺ ꟺ

For two years he worked like a man possessed. Although the *casco*, the ranch headquarters, was essentially like the headquarters of other *ranchos*, the mindset of the man who owned it was quite different.

Richard King regarded ranching as a business—not a lazy, somewhat easygoing way of life. He set out to conduct this business as he had conducted his steamboat business—for profit. Probably, he first saw his ranch as a way to increase his profits by providing raw materials for his steamboats to transport.

In those days the only marketable profits from cattle ranching were hides and tallow. The meat was largely unused because no way had been developed to move meat from the pasture to the big cities.

Before refrigeration, the cattle had to be herded over hundreds of miles, decreasing their value with every step. The length of time the live cow stayed on the trail or in the pen on board a steamboat directly reduced its weight. Also during that time, expenses to herders, handlers, shippers, and stockyards mounted.

King came from New York where mechanical refrigeration was being developed. Although such machines were unknown on the frontier, King must have anticipated a day when he could get his meat to market where the profit was.

During the extreme drought years of 1853 and 1854, the level of the Rio Grande sank until steamboat traffic was impossible north of Reynosa. This reduction in his trade must have spurred King to greater efforts in his ranching.

Meanwhile, the drought made him aware of the overall necessity for water. One of his first acts whenever he acquired a tract of land was to ascertain its water supply. By raising a dirt dam across the bed of Tranquitas Creek, a tributary of the Santa Gertrudis, King constructed the first engineering "improvement" between Brownsville and Corpus Christi. When the stream ran with rain, the water backed up into a lake that became the first place between the Nueces and the Arroyo Colorado where a thousand head of cattle could drink at one time.

As buildings and corrals were constructed, Legs Lewis and his Rangers furnished protection from marauders. The cowboys were still around, though not in such numbers. The Karankawas had been driven out long ago, but the Comanches, particularly the Pernatekas, the Quick Stingers, raided for horses to ride and eat, women to add to their importance, and children to become slaves.

While Lewis was in Corpus Christi and King was in Brownsville, Captain James Richardson, a veteran of the Mexican War, was hired as the first foreman of "King's *Rancho*." Under his educated eye, a stockade and blockhouse were constructed next to the seep spring where King had first camped. War surplus cannon from King's old steamboats were mounted on its ramparts as much to scare off marauders with their noise as to do them any damage.

One of the first men to work for King on horseback was the formidable Faustino Villa, whose prodigious strength and unquestioning loyalty made him invaluable to King. From the river he followed King to the ranch. There he became a straw boss and later *caporal* for King's *vaqueros*.

In 1854 King and Lewis began to buy their herds. They bought the best, paying better than top dollar. When cattle were selling for five dollars a head, King paid six and seven. Though he was never a rider, he coveted fine horses. Although he bought plenty of the cheap mustang stock, the early records mention horses like "the American gray stallion" for which he paid two hundred dollars and Whirlpool, a sorrel stud, six hundred dollars.

So determined was King to bring quality to his ranch that he spent twice as much money for a stud as he had paid for the first 15,500 acres.

The most revolutionary thing that King did was to lead an *entrada*. During the drought of 1853, he went into the dusty hills of Tamaulipas, south of the Rio Grande. The village of Cruillas disappeared on that very day and its name was forgotten for generations. The villagers' cattle and horses were exceptional, so King bought them all.

He was getting ready to drive them off when he realized now that he had bought all their cattle, the people living there were left with nothing to do.

He made them a proposition. Come and settle on the Santa Gertrudis. Build homes, work, get regular wages paid in cash. Persuaded by their *jefe* Francisco Alvarado, the village moved. One hundred men, women, and children with all they could pile on their rickety high-wheeled *carretas*, all they could pack on their *burros*, all they could pile on their wheelbarrows followed him out of their homeland.

They came down off the Eastern Mother Mountains. They forded the Big River. They marched across The Desert of the Dead. They followed him to the clear, fresh water of Saint Gertrude's Creek.

He became *El Senor Capitán* for the rest of his life. They became *Los Kineños*, the King People, the seeds of the most loyal group of people that ever worked for any man.

The Myth

The Ghost Horse

The Comanche came down off the Balcones in the spring of the year—the Moon When the Geese Lay Their Eggs. If the buffalo had not been late in coming from the north, they would never have ridden into the Wild Horse Desert looking for the thousands of animals they had heard roamed there.

But they were curious. The horse had become their way of life. They rode upon his back, they harnessed him to drag their tipis, they traded him to other tribes less able than they—for they were magical on horseback—and they ate his flesh when the buffalo drifted north in the summer.

From the deep grass the burning eyes of the Karankawas watched them. The Eaters of the Dead could only stare as the Quick Stingers rode by. Though taller and stronger, they dared not bother the horsemen. Of course, if a rider faltered or became lost from the rest, he could be pulled down and dispatched without harm. With that in their minds, the Karankawas followed the trail.

Together, the Comanche rode unchallenged with lances couched. Here and there prized eagle feathers lifted and twirled in the Gulf breeze. Buffalo-hide shields slapped gently against their horses' flanks.

And the Karankawas watched—and this is what they saw.

Not long into the sea of grass, the Comanches saw the plume of dust rising on the horizon. "Yah! Yah! Yah!" they cried, as they galloped toward it. Soon they came upon a band of horses grazing. They counted fine mares, many pregnant, many with colts at their flanks, yearlings, two-year-olds.

They had never seen so many horses all following a wild stallion. On a rise a distance away, a three-year-old stallion flung up his head and neighed shrilly. He was a steeldust roan with black mane and tail. No horse so young could have so many fine mares.

The Comanche recognized that he had been driven out—too old to be with the herd, too young to leave. He was an outcast. They nodded their heads. This was good, for the herd stallion would be very strong, very potent.

The riders further noted the horses were in unusually fine condition. Again they smiled to each other and grunted softly, "Hoh! Hoh!" The herd stallion must be a great one to take such good care of his band. They immediately decided that they must capture him.

They had moved closer to the herd before they saw him. When they did, their eyes widened, their hearts beat faster, their muscles tensed as blood raced through their veins. Galloping across the prairie toward them, his mane and tail sweeping behind him, came the most powerful horse they had ever seen.

He was unusually big, his steeldust hide covered with black and white hairs so finely intermixed that he glinted blue in the spring sun. They saw too that he differed from others of his kind, from his own son. His flowing mane and tail were silver.

Back and forth between the Indians and his herd, he dashed. He knew them as his enemies and by his actions warned them to come no closer.

The Karankawas watched and smiled thinly. They recognized the steeldust as he tore the ground to pieces in his anger at the intruders. Usually they gave his territory a wide berth. Now they watched—and waited hungrily—to see who would die in the tall grass of *El Desierto de los Muertos*.

Every man among the Comanche wanted to become his master. Every man imagined himself upon the stallion's back racing like the wind to kill the buffalo, breeding him to their best mares, and trading his colts for another wife.

The steeldust arched his fine neck and braced himself with his forelegs far out in front of him. Snorting and neighing, he threatened the warriors if they did not retreat. He showed them what he would do to them. He wagged his head furiously, tossing the silver mane into a froth. He leaped into the air and twisted his huge body, switching ends. His silver tail swirled. He reared up on his hind legs to paw the air. At last, he charged them, his teeth bared.

To show him who would be master, the Comanches charged toward him, yelling and brandishing their lances.

The steeldust reared again, screaming his defiance. His great hooves struck at the sun. Some of the horses of the Comanche faltered. What would happen if he didn't turn and run? They began to yell, brandishing their pinioned lances.

Finally, when they were galloping toward him from three sides, he wheeled on his strong hind legs and leaped away. His *ladina*, his lead mare, took the point, the band followed her, and he drove them before him nipping at their heels.

The yells of the Comanches filled the sky as they gave chase. Five miles, they followed him. And five miles more into a dry *arroyo*, whose walls were too steep for the herd to climb out. Some of the fleeter warriors galloped above him on the bank. Others warriors, fleeter still, galloped on ahead and dared death to ride their mounts down into the arroyo to head him off.

As the *ladina* saw her way blocked by screaming warriors, she turned aside and set the herd to milling.

Straight through their midst, the steeldust stormed. He plowed into several of his own, jostling them aside, knocking the little colts to the ground, trampling one of them. But he had no room to head his band up again, so he himself became trapped. Soon he couldn't be seen except for his silver mane tossing in the rising white dust stirred up by so many hooves.

"Yip-yip-yip, he-heeh-h-h!" the Comanches yelled. The cry of the prairie wolf rose on the banks and from both ends of the arroyo, signaling to each other. They had caught him, or so they believed.

Some of them climbed down off their horses and started toward the herd. They thought to capture the first mares for themselves, so they swung their ropes of braided rawhide.

Suddenly, with a mighty scream, the silver-maned stallion burst out of the mill. His long neck snaked forward, his hooves lanced out in front of his bared teeth.

The Comanche stood their ground, swinging their ropes, yelling; but he came like the hurricane. His hooves struck the nearest horse hunter and flung him to the ground. Swift as a cougar, the great horse wheeled and attacked, coming down on his victim's prone body with all four strong legs. The warrior's heart was crushed. He never drew another breath.

The second horse hunter tried to come to the aid of the first, but he was too late. He ran into the path of the steeldust's hind legs that kicked out, catching him beneath the chin. His neck snapped and he was thrown backward the full length of his body. He twitched once, then died.

The silver-maned stallion reared and whinnied, but the rest of the Comanches, who had frozen in amazement at the speed with which he had killed their comrades, now came alive. Calling to each other, they charged him with their lances couched as if he were a buffalo.

The watching Karankawas licked their lips as they counted those already dead in that arroyo.

The steeldust whirled once more and kicked his powerful hind legs into the face of one horse. His hard hooves sheared the meat from the side of its skull. The horse screamed and went down taking its rider with it. The stallion would have trampled him too, but the Comanches were upon him.

One stabbed his haunch with a lance, another rode in close enough to drive his iron point into the mighty shoulder.

With a scream of rage, the stallion whirled away toward the herd. They thought he would run in among the milling mares, but he was too clever. He knew unless he could burst free, he would be doomed. Rearing once more, he plunged forward, straight for the smallest Comanche mount. His broad chest struck the little mustang and sent it tumbling. Its rider went down, his leg trapped beneath his horse.

Whinnying shrilly, the steeldust leaped across the struggling bodies. Stretching out at full stride, he streaked out of the arroyo. None could catch him.

The Karankawas grinned as the half-hearted pursuit ceased and the Comanche rode back to bury their dead.

Had they but known they had created a killer, perhaps they would have ridden away faster than they did.

The first horse the steeldust encountered on his angry flight was the three-year-old. Challenging his own son, he tore the youngster's throat out with a single snap of his jaws. He galloped on, blood running from his shoulder and his haunch and the blood of his kills splashed across his chest and neck.

The Comanche finished their bad business as swiftly as might be. They buried their dead. They caught the mares and colts they wanted and left the others in the arroyo to be found or to find themselves another protector.

As the Comanche rode out, the Karankawas moved in to take what they would.

But that was not the end of the story. To their horror, the Comanche found the trail of the steeldust beast crossing their own throughout the Wild Horse Desert. The buzzards circling above marked his passage. He had gone mad now, killing every horse—mare or stallion—in his path.

But his real prey were the Comanche themselves.

When they camped for the night on a dry wash, from the darkness they felt the ground they lay upon tremble beneath them. They heard his shrill challenge and the thunder of his hooves. The wild mares and their colts threw up their heads. The horse hunters rolled out of their blankets and sought their lances.

But he did not come near. Instead, he stalked their camp, moving round it, stamping and snorting. Galloping in and then retreating. No one could sleep, so the Comanche broke camp before the dawn's light and fled back to the Staked Plains as if the devil himself were chasing them. They told their children his story and warned them never to go down into his land.

The steeldust became a legend. From the Nueces to the Rio Grande, men saw him on the rises in the moonlight shaking his wild silver crest. They found the bodies he had killed, bodies of his own kind and their kind.

The Karankawas followed where he led, but not too closely. Then they too deserted the desert, driven off by the Texans and the Mexicans. A century passed. The land became a great ranch.

Still the steeldust gallops through the night, wild and mad, a ghost horse, with moonlight glinting silver off his mane, and the *vaqueros* who are the *Kineños* mark his passing with the sign of the cross.

Part II

The Captain and His Lady

The Truth

La Patrona Arrives

The evening service of December 10, 1854, in the First Presbyterian Church in Brownsville was lighted by candles and lamps.

Miss Henrietta Chamberlain sat in her usual place in the choir. Her face was pale. Even though she looked exceptionally well, her hands must have trembled on the hymnal.

Captain Richard King sat in his much-less-than-usual place in the front pew. He wore a new suit and boots. He was freshly barbered and nervous.

His friend Mifflin Kenedy and Kenedy's wife sat beside him. Certainly, Charles Stillman was there. James O'Donnell as well as other riverboat captains of M. Kenedy and Co. enlarged the congregation as well as the faculty of the Rio Grande Female Institute where Henrietta taught.

At the end of the church service, the Reverend Hiram Chamberlain invited everyone present to attend the wedding service, which would begin immediately.

Instead of walking down the aisle, the bride came down from the choir. She looked—as all brides do—lovely, happy, excited, and a little frightened. Her new dress, made especially for the occasion, was more splendid than anything she had ever known. The gown of peach-colored ruffled silk had an inset front of white silk mull "shirred and trimmed with beading and white baby ribbons under sleeves of white lace."

The extravagance must have pricked the preacher's daughter's conscience. Her father had spent her whole life teaching her about the sins of pride and vanity. He had also spent many years teaching her to beware of the sins of the flesh.

His own letters after his marriage to her mother and her two stepmothers are almost apologetic when they point out how he is "indulging the passions of love." What did he say to her the night before she married? What references did he make to his favorite themes of "noble resolution" and "religious duty"? Did he enjoin her to remember that man is not "made to be *perfectly* happy here" on earth?

Yet here she was about to marry a man who cared neither for noble resolution nor religious duty. He wasn't a godly man at all, but he was a good man. She was absolutely sure of his goodness. As she smiled at him, she might have suspected that he was determined to make her perfectly happy.

Richard King rose and took her hand before the altar. Four years had passed since they'd first seen each other across the muddy waters of the Rio Grande, four years that rather than civilizing him had made him more the barbarian than ever. Becoming a man of means, acquiring all the wealth that came within his reach, he had become more ruthless as his goals became clearer. Henrietta was the wife on whom he had set his sights. In four years he had never faltered. To her credit, neither had she.

Hiram Chamberlain cleared his throat and solemnly wed his prim and proper daughter to the roistering riverboat captain and rancher from the Wild Horse Desert.

ꟿ ꟿ ꟿ

In November Richard King had paid four hundred dollars for a stagecoach. Even then good transportation cost money. That vehicle, which cost an additional twenty-five dollars to outfit, or one just like it is exhibited today in the King Ranch Museum.

King outfitted a stagecoach or "mudwagon" like this one to bring his bride to the Santa Gertrudis. (Author photo)

Even though King planned to build a house for them in town on Elizabeth Street next to Mifflin Kenedy, he couldn't wait to take her to their ranch, a honeymoon trip of over a hundred miles.

Of course, he wanted her to be as comfortable as possible. He still wasn't a good rider. He much preferred a stagecoach even when it meant jouncing over the prairies where roads trailed off into a pair of ruts with the grass and weeds worn low between them.

They started out the next day pulled by a team of four powerful horses. Beside the driver sat an armed guard. Thirty heavily armed outriders with the look of *bandidos* from the hills of Tamaulipas rode before and after to protect the couple from attacks by bandits or Indians. They had been chosen from among the *Kineños* who had followed King out of Mexico.

Faustino Villa undoubtedly rode among them, grinning with pride at his captain's choice.

The groom had planned a quick trip because he was eager to show his new wife what their future would be like. Even though he had bought a house in Brownsville, the ranch was to be their eventual home. The journey took four days. Thirty miles a day was an ordeal over the route they had to travel. In the wake of the two-year drought, white caliche dust rose from beneath the horses' hooves and covered the coach.

King had also planned the journey as a sort of honeymoon. Camps had been set up along the way. A ranch cook waited at each stop to prepare the meals. Fresh outriders replaced the ones who had ridden with them during the day. These stood guard during the night while the others slept.

The bride must have looked out at the desolate countryside and wondered what she was doing there amid brown grass, gray mesquite, and thorny cactus. At night the leaping flames of the campfires and the coals of the cook fire would have little to press back the great dark vault of the

Texas skies. Even the thousands of stars overhead must have seemed far, far away—the moon, a huge cold ball.

Inside their tent after all was quiet, Henrietta lay on their iron cot and listened to the creatures rustling in the dark. Armadillos waddled and snuffled about in the thickets rooting for grubs. Nighthawks and bats dipped and fluttered across the moon on their perpetual hunt for insects. Screech owls hooted from the oak motte, frightening timid mice and rabbits into fleeing. Coyotes sang their night songs that sound like a demented chorus to a young stranger who's never heard them before. A band of wild horses galloped across the horizon setting the ground to vibrating beneath her.

She was traveling through another world, as different from Brownsville as Brownsville had been from Tennessee. This time she wasn't going with her father but with a relative stranger. What's more, she couldn't go back if the world made her unhappy. She'd made her vows before the altar and before God.

Before they got close enough to see the house, a band of *vaqueros* came riding out to meet them led by Captain Legs Lewis. King rolled up the leather curtains inside the coach so his bride could see and be seen.

Mexican *vaqueros* are invariably gallant, invariably eager to show off. What dashing riders they must have made! How they must have jerked their hats off in broad sweeping circles as they rode past grinning, their white teeth flashing beneath their black moustaches!

They were all very flattering, very complimentary.

Then she caught her first sight of the *rancho*. If she kept her face serene, she must have been made of stern stuff indeed. Under bare December trees on the rise by the seep spring stood a cluster of earth-brown wattled huts and a thatch-roofed commissary. They were all the *Kineños* had been able to construct with the limited lumber of Wild Horse Desert.

Horses in shaggy winter coats occupied the corrals. But what poor-looking corrals they were. Gray tangles of twisted mesquite limbs sunk side by side into the earth, their jagged ends making a snaggletoothed barricade. Dominating everything was a blockhouse and a stockade from which the mouths of brass cannon thrust threateningly. The very presence of those cannon installed at that fort told a story more succinct than words.

As they approached, the *vaqueros* galloped past the coach and swung down. Eager but shy, smiling but diffident, from everywhere King's people came out to greet her, to sweep their hats off deferentially, to curtsy, to bow low to her as if she were royalty inspecting her troops.

She was.

She was a queen named King. She was *La Patrona*. She was *La Madonna*. As she remembers it, she fell in love all over again with every one of them. Seeing them so happy, she knew what she had been born for. She had a flock to care for. She looked up at her Captain and smiled. She had a King to make a king.

ʍ ʍ ʍ

The ranch "house" was a *jacál*, a hut made with upright poles covered with mud and smoothed to look somewhat like adobe. It was no different from the ones the rest of the people lived in, only a little bigger and a little smoother-sided. The pantry was so small she had to hang her big serving platters on the outside wall. It had a dirt floor.

Lumber to build a big house was already contracted for. It only waited for her direction. To please his bride was what King wanted more than anything.

He called her Etta and, when they were alone, Pet. She called him Captain. She'd first seen him on the deck of a steamboat. She'd thought of him as her Captain for four years. By her own account, their honeymoon was the happiest any bride might wish for.

All that mild winter and early spring they roamed the prairie on horseback, seeing the wonders of it, the grass, the thickets where all manner of strange birds lived, the roadrunners, the scissor-tails, the ubiquitous buzzards, so different from pretty robin red-breasts and blue jays.

When she tired, he'd spread a Mexican blanket for her and she'd take her siesta under the shade of a mesquite tree, dappled shade, the tiny leaves like fern fronds.

She wrote to her grandfather in far, far away Vermont that she had found "a mate of congenial tastes and sympathies." The modest description represented a prodigious understatement of her joy.

ʊʊ ʊʊ ʊʊ

In every way, she began the business of Christianizing and civilizing everything in sight—her husband included. Temperance was one of her abiding dictates. No one on the ranch was to drink whiskey or mescal on the ranch. From then on the men had to hide their liquor carefully and take drinks only when they were sure she was nowhere around.

She took charge of everyone on the place, nursing the sick and supplying the needy. Everyone was expected to attend church services every Sunday. The people adored her.

Bandits came to know her as well. The word among them was that it was better to approach the house when *El Capitán* was there than when *La Patrona* was by herself. With *El Capitán* a man might make a deal. When she was alone and in charge, a man didn't have a chance.

Her reputation grew not through any harshness or sternness on her part. Indeed she never refused a stranger. All who came were welcome. The word was that she would have tried to reform any miscreant who happened by.

Furthermore, no one dared to try to harm her or rob her. The *Kineños* held her in such high esteem they would willingly have died for her. Rather than do so, they made certain that anyone who might harm her died first.

Even before the ranch house was completed, her hospitality was known in Corpus Christi. People came to visit and stay.

Assuming the duties of hostess with an eye to bringing grace and manners to her captain's house, she insisted that everyone at least make a show of dressing for dinner even when everyone still ate in the commissary. Sometimes all the show a drifter could muster might be washing his hands and face and brushing the dust off his clothing, but it was still the rule.

ꟺ ꟺ ꟺ

Her efforts to bring civilization to the *rancho* were curtailed after the middle of the year. King took her back to Brownsville to a cottage on Elizabeth Street next door to his friends the Kenedys.

She was expecting their first child.

The Bureaucracy Takes Notice

What *La Patrona* thought of handsome, reckless, Captain Gideon K. "Legs" Lewis is unknown. Strict Presbyterian that she was she couldn't have approved of a known drinker and philanderer. Still, she probably kept her mouth firmly closed. He was her husband's friend and business partner. At thirty, a year younger than Richard King, he was famous throughout Texas for his heroism during the Mexican War. He had been a soldier first and later a Texas Ranger.

In January he had decided to follow Richard King's example to become a solid citizen. He planned to run for Congress from the Nueces District.

On April 14, 1855, an irate husband shot him dead.

On April 17 the same husband wrote a letter of apology to Captain King. In it he explained his motive succinctly and took care to inform King that, although he was with the sheriff and bound for Galveston, he was "free of all bonds."

The *Galveston Journal* gave a further account. Lewis had seduced Doctor J. T. Yarrington's wife and persuaded her to leave him. Unfortunately for Lewis's reputation, the doctor had intercepted letters that explicitly incriminated the would-be politician. Legs came twice to get them. The doctor refused and promised to shoot Legs if the former Ranger came back. When Legs appeared for the third time, the doctor opened the door and shot him with a double-barreled shotgun.

Lewis's morals notwithstanding, King had lost not only a good friend but also a business partner. That partnership immediately created problems which cost the ranch a great deal of money and for a time threatened its very existence.

Legs Lewis died without a will and without any heirs. Eventually, a succession of three different court-appointed administrators were required to settle his properties, which included interest in both the *Rincón* and the *De la Garza Santa Gertrudis* land grants. Of course, their value was difficult to determine.

The land was certainly more valuable than when he and King bought it, but how much had it been improved? What was the value of a blockhouse and stockade, mesquite corrals, and a cluster of *jacales*? What was the value of Mexican cattle and *vaqueros* and their families?

At that time King could not have been in a worse position to pay out cash money. As a result of the two-year-long drought, the Rio Grande was so low that steamboats could go no farther than Rio Grande City. After buying a new steamer, *Ranchero*, he and Kenedy were unable to use her. His income from M. Kenedy and Co. was greatly reduced. In fact, it was nonexistent.

His desire to secure the ranch became an absolute necessity at this time, yet his prospects were bleak. Within a year he'd become a family man with responsibilities, and within a year he'd been saddled with debts. Selling part of the new ranch—a prospect that went against everything he believed in—was a distinct possibility.

He was financially insolvent. He had spent lavishly for his wedding. He was building a brick house on Elizabeth Street in Brownsville. Henrietta was about to give birth to their first child. Baby Henrietta, whom they called Nettie, was born April 17, 1856. Loving his wife and his child, King knew his solitary life was over forever, but how he must have worried about his financial situation.

Legs's share of the *Rincón de Santa Gertrudis* went up for public sale on July 1, 1856. Desperate to avoid having a partner who didn't share his goals, King made arrangements with a friend. Major W. W. Chapman represented King in the sale. Even though Chapman had been instructed to top any bid, he felt he'd been forced to pay a larger sum than either man had anticipated. Interest was building in the new ranching effort forty-five miles from Corpus Christi. Speculators began to look hard and long at the land if for no other reason than to see what King saw in it. The gavel fell on the sum of $1,575 payable by notes due one year from the date of purchase.

The piece of land for which King had paid three hundred dollars in 1853 was worth more than three thousand in 1856 even after two years of drought.

More trouble came only a few days later when the U.S. Army transferred Major Chapman to California. With his possible partner gone, King was left to pay the entire note himself. That he was late in paying is a matter of record, but he did eventually pay it.

The trouble with the *De la Garza Santa Gertrudis* was even more complicated. King and Lewis had never paid any money for it. Because of the delays of the Matamoros real estate agent Manuel Elisondo, the documents had never been proved. Though King and Lewis had paid for proving, they had never gotten clear title to it.

King had to take in another partner, James Walworth, a steamboat captain. Together they went directly to Praxides Uribe, who hired another agent. His price too had gone up considerably in two and a half years. Instead of the eighteen hundred dollars listed in the original contract, Walworth had to pay five thousand.

King was furious with frustration. Everything had seemed settled only a year ago. Now everything was in turmoil.

Interest in the Wild Horse Desert was suddenly burgeoning. In Brownsville as in Corpus Christi, businessmen were looking north toward Wild Horse Desert and seeing a hazy vision of what King had seen the first time Lewis had led him across it.

Dealing with what amounted to blackmail, King came to realize that his success was attracting the attention of greedy Johnny-come-latelies. He began a practice that stood him and the ranch in good stead all the rest of his life. He retained the very best lawyer he could find to handle his legal matters.

He chose Stephen Powers of Brownsville for the job.

Powers understood the importance of friends in high places. He had been a friend of Zachary Taylor. He had powerful connections in Washington. Among his friends were Martin Van Buren, James K. Polk, Franklin Pierce, and Millard Fillmore. Among his friends in Austin were Sam Houston and Thomas J. Rusk.

Powers took King under his wing. What began as a business relationship became friendship that lasted all their lives. With Powers as his sponsor, the runaway apprentice from New York began to hobnob with Brownsville's affluent and well connected, dubbed the Brick House Crowd. Although Henrietta didn't attend most functions, pleading her family and her church, King was seen about in the society of army functions and galas in Matamoros.

In choosing a law firm and retaining it, King set a new standard for the business of big ranching. Such a thing had never been done before. Ranchers tended to be solitary entities, keeping their own counsel and having as few dealings as possible with people who lived in towns and cities. When an emergency arose with regard to business, they were vulnerable to cheaters and swindlers.

King knew he was ill prepared for dealing with the legal system. He chose Powers to handle contracts and negotiations for him. As a result he was never at the mercy of the law. With King's success other ranchers took note and began to ape his dealings.

ᴡ ᴡ ᴡ

The rains came in the middle of 1856, and M. Kenedy & Co. had a surge of business. They were able to navigate their new steamer *Ranchero* upriver and show a profit over what she had cost them the year before. Army contracts came their way.

King had to spend more time in Brownsville away from his beloved ranch. He'd learned another valuable lesson. He saw the need to diversify his business so he'd never be at the mercy of the weather again. At that time he became a purveyor of goods as well as a transporter. He signed contracts with the army for mules, horses, and feed.

Among his army friends was a man he came to admire. While *Ranchero* steamed away from Rio Grande City, King met the officer who had just come aboard bound downriver for Fort Brown. Captain King and Lieutenant Colonel Robert E. Lee took to each other immediately.

King had found someone he could truly respect and emulate. Lee was seventeen years older and just the sort to be an older brother and adviser. Shortly after he had settled in at Fort Brown, Lee and some of his junior officers paid a formal call at the King home on Elizabeth Street.

King was away at the time, but Mrs. King extended the hospitality she was famous for and invited them to dinner.

Lee refused. He was too much of a gentleman to do as many army officers did when they showed up at dinnertime in hopes of getting an invitation.

Though Lee didn't dine at the brick house that night, he dined there many times during the five years he was stationed at Fort Brown. He loved Brownsville where he often walked along the river. He commented on the orange trees and the banks of flowers. He took rides with King and several times rode north to be entertained at the Santa Gertrudis.

Delighted to be entertaining so gallant a gentleman at the ranch, Henrietta swore that the lieutenant colonel enjoyed the dinner served off tin plates in the dining hall as much or more than he enjoyed it in their dining room on Elizabeth Street.

Owning his own estate back in Virginia gave Lee rich experience with things agrarian. He was impressed with the boundless grass and impressed with King's prospects of purchasing more land. His own state was full of people, and land was expensive. His advice to King was, "Buy land, and never sell."

ꟽ ꟽ ꟽ

The family's trips to the ranch were now conducted quite differently from the wedding journey. They left early in the morning or after dark and traveled all night in their stagecoach. As the Santa Gertrudis drew more attention, more people began to trickle into Wild Horse Desert. Rustlers and bandits came, eager to steal what they were too lazy to earn by honest work.

Faustino Villa was likely along on every trip the little family made. He was a truly big man and brave as a lion. His reputation was formidable, and the sight of him would send lesser men scurrying out of his way.

Indians too were still a threat. One day Mrs. King was baking bread in the *jacál*. Nettie was in her cradle by the door where she'd be cool. Her mother turned to see a half-naked Indian standing on the threshold. When Henrietta faced him, he moved to the cradle and stood over it brandishing a club.

Henrietta knew the threat to her child was absolutely real. Screaming or attempting to fight him would probably have gotten them both killed. Guessing that he wanted the fresh-baked bread, Mrs. King grabbed up all the loaves she had and thrust them against his chest. While she scooped up the baby, he disappeared out the door.

~ ~ ~

In late 1857 and early 1858 the "original" ranch house was built. Tradition has that the site for the house was suggested by Robert E. Lee. The family moved in, expanded by the addition of King's second daughter. On April 13, 1858, Ella Morse King was born in Brownsville.

The house was a story-and-a-half frame structure with an attic under its high-peaked roof—quite different from the flat-roofed adobe *jacál*. It had jalousied windows on all sides. Six-columned porches or galleries stretched the width of both front and back. Made of second-hand lumber purchased when the army abandoned the depot and post at Corpus Christi, the materials were hauled the forty-five miles overland by oxcart.

The kitchen and dining room were in a separate building as most were in those days. Set apart, they ensured that the main dwelling wouldn't be uncomfortably heated by the cook fires, nor would it be set on fire by accidents in the kitchen.

The carriage house proclaims the founding date 1853
and the date of incorporation 1909.
(Author photo)

In the midst of all this building for the family, carpenters were instructed to build a one-room schoolhouse. Like every Presbyterian since John Knox founded the church, Henrietta King believed in education. The children of the *Kineños* began their lessons under the eye of *La Patrona*, who had given up her position at the Rio Grande Female Institute when she married.

As King's family grew, so did his herds of horses and cattle. The first sales receipts were from horse sales. Even though the captain was a poor rider, he loved good horseflesh. Horses and mules were necessities in nineteenth-century Texas. The market was always high dollar.

At first, with boundless acres on all sides, the stock were allowed to roam free. That practice soon had to change. Mexican bandits drifted up across the border, and Texan rustlers drifted down across the Nueces. Sometimes these bands would attack the ranch house. Sometimes a bullet shot from a lone gunman would come whistling by.

And so the feudal system whereby the lord protected his people, who had sworn allegiance to him, came into being in South Texas. King had to protect his people. By the commissary he had a watchtower constructed. How tall the original one was is unknown, but the one that stood above the second ranch house was seventy-five feet tall and manned at all times. The ranch house today, which looks something like a Spanish palace, has a tower that provides a view for miles around.

The commissary where hundreds of Kineños, visitors, and strangers were fed. No one was ever turned away. (Author photo)

In this manner King saw that no one executed a surprise attack on his people. Still the rustling went on. He began to develop brands. His first brand was the *Ere Flecha*. It was never used on live cattle but burned into the hides he sold.

On March 20, 1859, he registered his first live cattle brand at the brand registry in Nueces County in the name of "Mistress Henrietta M. King, wife of Richard King." It was the first brand registered to the King Ranch.

Other brands followed until King devised the famous Running which became the superseding mark. Ever after, Henrietta lived happily content knowing that hers was first, a tribute to how much he loved her and wanted her to be part of everything he ever did and all he ever owned.

As the ranch became more famous, men came to buy cattle, to sell fine horses, to travel through and sample the famous hospitality. King built a men's dormitory beside the commissary. Still when the men ate with the family in the stone kitchen, every man from the wealthy to the poor was expected to dress for dinner. King's "Pet" seemed determined to civilize the entire country.

With her at his side, King was more determined than ever to make their ranch the most successful in the world.

	Ere Flecha brand, first used by King on hides
HK	HK brand, first brand registered to the King Ranch (1859)
	Running W brand, currently used

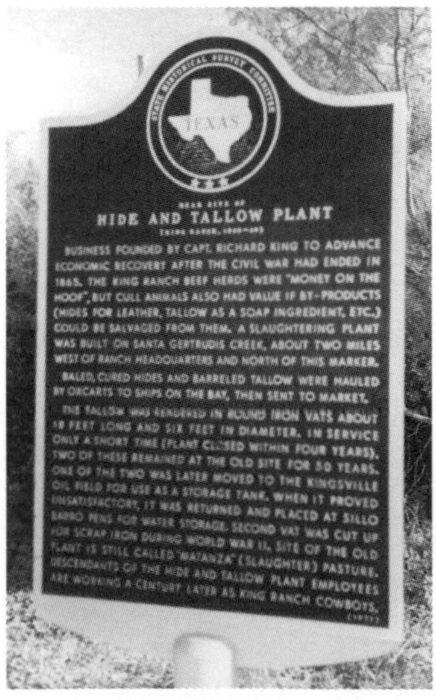

This historical marker describes early industry on the King Ranch. (Author photo)

Strife on the Border

In 1858 the government of Mexico created a free trade zone six miles wide along the entire northern frontier of the State of Tamaulipas. In this zone goods could be imported from foreign countries free of duty. The idea was to encourage trade.

The next year General D. E. Twiggs, commander of the Department of Texas, ordered all United States troops away from the border. His idea was to facilitate freedom of movement back and forth between the two nations.

What happened was that law enforcement was weakened on both sides of the Rio Grande. Only local officials in Matamoros and Brownsville claimed any responsible jurisdiction, and two nationalities that had fought a bloody war only twenty-two years before faced each other across a suddenly narrowing river.

The average American was more prosperous because he paid more attention to "prosperity" than the average Mexican. Furthermore, the land north of the river comprised its delta. The black alluvial soil stretched from Camargo southward toward the Gulf. It was much richer than the comparable land on the south side of the river. Combined with a 360-day growing season and frequent rainfall, the relatively small triangle that today comprises Cameron, Willacy, Hidalgo, and Starr Counties was some of the richest land on the continent of North America.

Jealousies raged in the hearts of businessmen and farmers on the south side of the border. Mexicans looked at the flourishing crops and herds and remembered that the land should have been theirs.

ᏇᏇᏇ

Naturally, the more powerful and wealthier Richard King and Mifflin Kenedy became, the more envied they were. And the more detractors they garnered. Even though they owned no land in the delta, they were making their living there.

King in particular drew malicious accusations from all sides.

His rivals accused him of operating a monopoly and charging exorbitant rates for his riverboats. (The weak point in the argument was that wagon train rates were higher than riverboat rates.) Suits were brought against him from time to time, but his friend and colleague Stephen Powers, the smartest lawyer in Brownsville, handled them.

He was no longer simply transporting people and goods on the Rio Grande. He had bought the boundless acres of Wild Horse Desert, the land nobody else wanted, and was fast turning it into an empire. On it he raised the horses and hides that he himself transported. Furthermore, he sold horses, mules, and cattle to buyers whom he then charged to transport the animals up or down the river.

Most unforgivable, his rivals could see how they could have done it too. King, they said, had been too clever. Or too quick. Or too lucky.

Like a colossus, King stood in the eye of the gathering political storm.

Brownsville was sharply divided between the "Reds," as the Democrats were called, and the "Blues," the Republicans. Emotions at election time were hot. King, a Democrat, was a strong proponent of States' Rights. In the off year elections, however, more Republicans were gaining seats in the U.S. Congress and Senate.

The possibility existed that a Republican might even be president after the 1860 election. If that happened, powerful men all over the South were talking openly of secession.

Richard King's feelings about seceding from the Union are unknown. Certainly, he believed in States' Rights, but he was born in New York City. His wife came from Vermont. His partners Kenedy and Stillman were from Pennsylvania and New York respectively. A war would certainly interfere with their plans. A war could possibly destroy their profitable business altogether. The chances are good that he was not in favor of it. Besides he had more immediate problems to worry about.

~ ~ ~

Between the Rio Grande and the Nueces in 1859, the most serious rivalry existed not between Northerners and Southerners, but between Americans and Mexicans in Matamoros and elsewhere along the Rio Grande. The Nueces Strip, as the Wild Horse Desert was being referred to, was becoming more and more the focus of a vendetta among Mexicans eager to reclaim what Zachary Taylor had won and their government in Mexico City had sold and signed away.

To this day the King Ranch carries a reputation for having taken advantage of the misfortunes of others. Much of that criticism comes from this era. While Kenedy and Co. rushed to consolidate their positions and put their wealth in safe investments, some people chose to believe themselves cheated.

They found it convenient to believe that Richard King and other ranchers like him had somehow managed to swindle them out of their grants.

The Rio Grande valley became an area without law; stripped of protection, the ranches to the north were open to rustlers, thieves, and murderers.

King had taken his family out to the Santa Gertrudis as the troubles in Brownsville heated. Even more than a hundred miles away seemed too little as the bandits and rustlers became bolder and bolder. The watchtower was manned constantly. The *Kineños* rode heavily armed and in pairs.

Even as this was happening, King took his family on a trip to enroll Henrietta's younger half brother in Centre College in Danville, Kentucky. While they were there, King bought some blooded Kentucky horses and good shorthorn cattle for shipment to Texas. He also began fencing in his range with lumber traded for cattle. Though the ranch lost hundreds of head of stock to rustlers in the next five years, King never ceased to make improvements that increased its size and wealth.

ꟿ ꟿ ꟿ

The most famous rascal among the bandits of the Nueces Strip was Juan Nepomuceno Cortinas. "Cheno" was red-haired and green-eyed, more Spaniard than Mexican, with a desperate hatred of all things American and Texan. He gathered a troop of admirers and adventurers and raided town after town. No one was safe. Although he never rode as far north as the Santa Gertrudis, he didn't spare the riverboats of M. Kenedy and Company.

After a year of his depredations, with the U.S. government unwilling to stop him, Texas sent a Ranger troop led by one of its most famous members. Captain John Salmon Ford came back to South Texas where he had gained a name for himself during the Mexican War.

Texans everywhere were glad to see him come. He was known to be a hard man, but a fair one, and a fierce fighter. His nickname was almost as famous as he was. He had signed Rest In Peace above his name at the end of his casualty reports during the Mexican War. As the lists grew longer and the war more heated, he was reduced to using the initials. Thereafter and forever, his men and the rest of Texas called him "Old Rip."

At the end of January 1860 Ford managed to corner Cortinas.

King's riverboat *Ranchero* was carrying $300,000 in gold bullion and specie from Rio Grande City to Brownsville. Ford's Rangers and two troops of cavalry used the gold as bait to lure Cortinas onto the riverbank. The Rangers outflanked him and charged. Cortinas fled to fight another day.

ᏔᏔᏔ

In March 1860 word came that Lieutenant Colonel Robert E. Lee was to be sent back to San Antonio as commander of the Department of Texas of the United States Army. His transfer to a command of such importance was surprising, for he was a Southerner. Sentiment against them was running high in government circles.

King and Kenedy welcomed the news. He was an old friend and a brave man, not like the ineffectual Twiggs who had left the border undefended. They were hopeful that his Southern sympathies would smooth the way for Texas in what was to come.

In November 1860, before Lee could arrive, Abraham Lincoln, a Republican, was elected president of the United States with nearly all his votes coming from the northern states. The Democratic party split its votes among three candidates. The election was infamous in American history, for it marked the first time that a president had been elected without a majority of the popular vote.

National disaster could no longer be forestalled. Believing that war was inevitable, King and Kenedy knew they would no longer be able to purchase riverboats for their fleet. Nowhere south of the border were there boat builders whose crafts would meet their requirements.

For both men business was uppermost in their minds. Kenedy immediately made plans to leave for Pittsburg, Pennsylvania, to buy a new boat, which they had already decided would be named the *Matamoros*. Knowing that a war in the Unites States would be a signal to Mexicans like Cortinas to try to take back the Wild Horse Desert, Kenedy sold his land at San Salvador del Tule across the Rio Grande from Camargo.

Kenedy was relieved to be rid of it because Cortinas had already stolen and scattered most of his stock. What animals remained he ordered his *vaqueros* to drive north to the Santa Gertrudis and mix them in the herds there. In so doing, he became a partner with King in the ranching business and placed his property out of harm's way if civil war came.

Meanwhile, Richard King rode south to Brownsville to set Stephen Powers to work to register the titles—his, his wife's, Kenedy's, and Walworth's—under a ranching partnership. The new firm established on December 5, 1860, was styled R. King & Co. At the same time King began making arrangements to close the house on Elizabeth Street and set up headquarters on the ranch.

He had planned to return to get Henrietta, but in early December she was afraid to remain longer in the comparative safety of the ranch. She had to get to her doctor in Brownsville. Her cortege started out.

December 15, 1860, Richard King II was born, according to his own account, "in a stagecoach while Mother was hurrying to Brownsville."

After two little princesses, a prince was born to the King and his queen of what was to become a very troubled kingdom.

ꟷ ꟷ ꟷ

Within days after Abraham Lincoln was inaugurated on March 4, 1861, Ranger Ben McCulloch, as military commander representing the rebel convention in Austin, led an armed force into San Antonio.

Confronted with the steely-eyed McCulloch, a truly formidable man, Major General Twiggs surrendered without protest. When Lieutenant Colonel Robert E. Lee arrived in the afternoon, the coup was already accomplished and Twiggs was leaving.

Lee shook his head sadly. "Has it come already?" he asked. He never assumed his post.

While the U.S. troops were being evacuated north, fifteen hundred Texas troops marched to the Rio Grande, there to be commanded by the newly commissioned Colonel Rip Ford. Although the war had already begun, King saw hope in Ford's command. At least the border would be defended.

Texas hearts everywhere swelled with pride at the sight of the Lone Star flying over Ringgold Barracks at Fort Brown.

The Myth

La Llorona

The son of a rich *hidalgo,* a nobleman of pure Spanish blood saw the young woman as she bent her head beneath her shawl at mass. With the candle glow silhouetting her delicate features, he was struck by her beauty.

In the bright sunlight outside the mission, he saw her for what she was, a *mestizo,* one of mixed blood, half Spanish, half Indian. As the scion of his family, he could never make an alliance, let alone a marriage, with her, but he reasoned that he would treat her well and leave her with more than she had when he first saw her.

Therefore, he approached her, bowed low, and asked her to walk with him. She raised her eyes to his face. The sun highlighted the gold of his hair and glided gently over his smooth skin. To say she was dazzled was to seriously understate the attraction she felt.

Flattered beyond belief at the handsome young man's attention, she fell like a ripe fruit into his careless hands. With a few soft words, a few caresses, a gentle kiss, he won her love. He himself recognized the depth of her passion. It flattered him and he told himself that all was going exactly as he had planned.

He caused a *haciendita* to be built for her farther down the arroyo from his parents' much larger, more elaborate home. In this way he isolated her from friends and family. She could no longer go to the mission unless he himself took her.

Innocent and unquestioning, she gladly did all that he asked of her. In the course of time, she bore him two sons, both of whom he could never deny, for their hair was the true Castilian gold and their skin was smooth and fair.

One day as he prepared to leave the *haciendita*, he asked her to walk out with him. Her heart beat fast, for she knew what he would say was most important. She thought of a reaffirmation of their love. She thought shyly of marriage.

He announced that his father had heard of their affair and was sending him back to Spain. There he would marry a woman of his own class, one who was rich and properly educated, one whom he could lead on his arm with pride. He saw the color drain from her face. Her lips became seamed like those of an old woman.

Seeking to soften the blow, he told her that since his intended had been chosen by his family, he did not expect to be happy.

He saw her whole body tremble as the heart within her breast set up a frantic beating.

He would do what was right and proper, he assured her. With that he turned to mount his horse, but she caught hold of the bridle and begged him to stay but one minute.

From the little house, she carried out his two sons, beautiful boys with golden hair and fair skin, the skin of a *hidalgo*, rather than a *mestizo*. "What will you do with them?" she asked through her tears. "They are so young, so fair. How can your heart not break?"

"I will take them with me," he announced coldly.

She couldn't believe her ears. These were her sons too. They were the light of her life. Her entire existence was built on loving and caring for them and for him. For the first time she understood that he had no thought of her as a person. She was a possession. He cared for her no more than his horse or his hounds. Indeed, he must have thought less of her than of his horses and dogs. He thought her incapable of love.

Shrieking in fury at his revelation, she flung herself at him. Her boys fled in terror before this creature, who they no longer recognized as their mother. The *hidalgo* also fell back before her fury, but too late. Her nails raked flesh from his cheeks. Blood ran down and dripped onto his white shirt, his white linen shirt into which she had set each stitch with loving hands.

Cursing, he shoved her away. When she tried to lunge at him again, he struck her to the ground. He raised his whip, but her fury had turned against her own innocence. As one gone mad, she clawed at her own face.

He climbed on his stallion and stared down at her prostrate figure as if he had never seen her before. She looked up, her hatred bright in her eyes.

"I'll come back when you are more yourself," he said. He struggled to keep the loathing from his voice, but she heard it clearly. His cheeks still dripped blood. She saw it trickle down his neck.

"Have the boys ready to go. They will be reared as my first sons. I promise you that."

She scrambled up from the dust and ran into the *haciendita* he had built for her, the place where they had been so happy. While her own blood still dripped, she donned the white dress, the one she wore when he came to her the first time.

It had been like a bridal dress, for she loved him so much that she thought surely his love for her made this union as sanctified as any rite that a priest had performed.

Now, it would do to bury her.

She let her hair down, her long black hair that fell below her hips. How she had trembled when he ran his fingers through it and kissed her!

With her smile fixed upon her lips, she walked toward the arroyo.

Her sons crept out from behind the jasmine at the side of the *haciendita* and followed her. They spoke to her and tugged at her dress, but she did not answer them.

She was thinking furiously. No one could rear them as she would. They would be helpless and abused without her. Better a quick easy death.

At the bank of the arroyo she paused. The brown water swirled and eddied more than half a dozen yards beneath her feet. The clay bank was steep and slippery. Nothing that fell into it could ever climb out.

She thought no more. Lifting each child in one arm and settling them astraddle each hip in the time-honored way of loving mothers, she jumped.

Together they sank like a single stone.

The *hidalgo* returned to find the *haciendita* empty and his children gone. He searched. He called her name. He sent his men to search.

Night fell. They returned with the drowned bodies of the two small sons. They did not find her body. It must have caught in the roots at the muddy bottom.

The *hidalgo* buried his sons, burned the *haciendita*, and returned to Spain, where he married the rich woman who was the choice of his family. He never smiled again. And she gave him no children.

The girl in the white dress ascended into Heaven.

The Master at the Gate told her that because of her suffering, she could enter. She had only to return with the souls of her sons. Since she had carried them to their deaths, she must carry them to their eternal peace.

Weeping, she turned away to search for them.

But she cannot find the *haciendita*, only ashes. She cannot find their bodies. She does not know the *hidalgo* has buried them.

To this day on the Arroyo Colorado, the Arroyo Hondo, Los Olmos Creek, and even the Santa Gertrudis Creek, *La Llorona*, the Weeping Woman, sweeps the bank with her long hair. She puts her long stick fingers into the muddy bottoms and searches for the bodies of her children. When she cannot find them, her weeping is inconsolable.

People walking by the water at night hear her distinctly. They hold their children's hands tighter and hurry by with heads turned. Once in their *jacales*, their *casas*, their *ranchitos*, they take their children's faces between their palms and speak solemnly to them.

"Never go near the river at night. Never. Never. Never. *La Llorona* is there. She is searching for her own children, but it has been years, centuries since she saw them. She is mad. She may mistake you for one of them.

"If she did, she would take you away—forever."

Part III

Ruffle of Drums

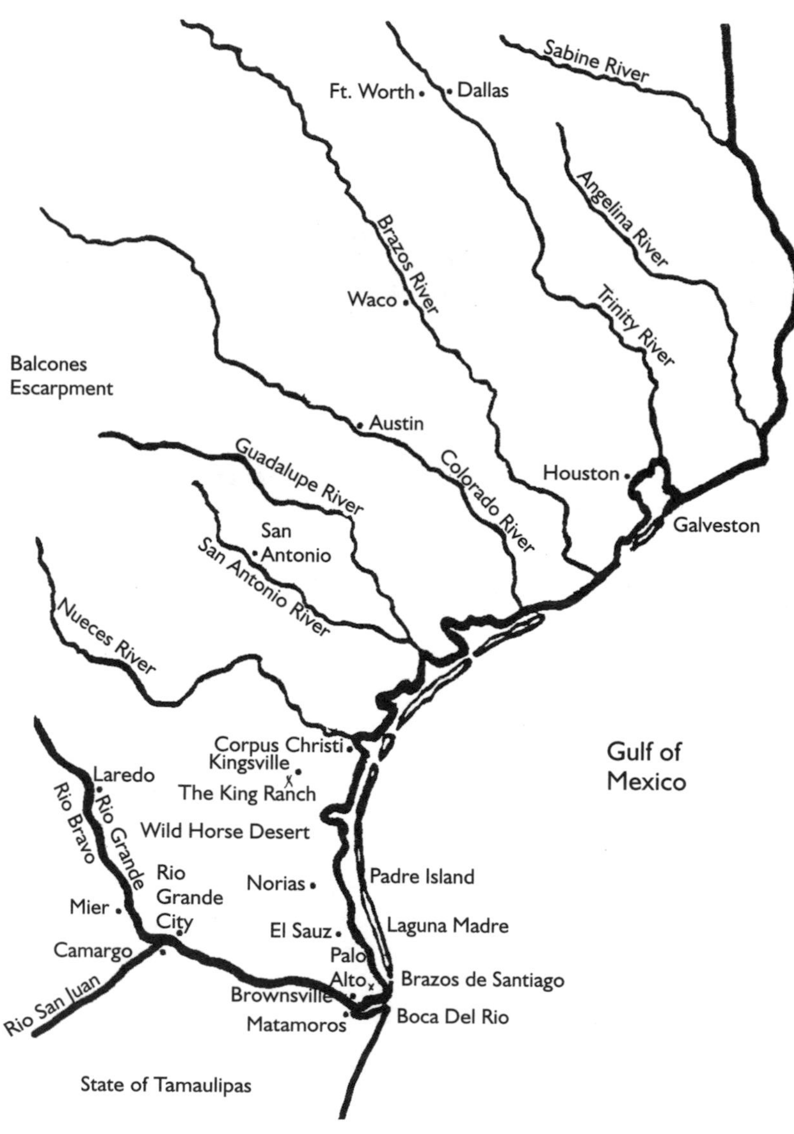
Sabine River
Ft. Worth
Dallas
Angelina River
Brazos River
Waco
Trinity River
Balcones
Escarpment
Austin
Colorado River
Houston
Guadalupe River
Galveston
San
Antonio
San Antonio River
Nueces River
Corpus Christi
Kingsville
Gulf of
Mexico
Laredo
The King Ranch
Rio Bravo
Rio Grande
Wild Horse Desert
Rio
Grande
City
Norias
Padre Island
Mier
El Sauz
Laguna Madre
Camargo
Palo
Alto
Brazos de Santiago
Rio San Juan
Brownsville
Matamoros
Boca Del Rio
State of Tamaulipas

The Truth

The Rebel Agent

On April 12, 1861, Fort Sumter was fired upon. A bloody conflict—the most costly the United States ever fought—was joined. It would not cease until the South lay broken and bleeding, its finest young men slaughtered and its economy in ruins.

Fifteen days later Lincoln proclaimed a blockade of all southern ports. King Cotton, worth thousands of dollars in the factories of England and France, was effectively trapped and much of the South's military capabilities with it. Without the money the cotton would have provided, the southern states had nothing with which to buy their armaments. Stupidly unprepared, the citizens of the Confederate States of America gave all they could to the Cause and lost most of what they had left.

Such was not the case with King and Kenedy. Therein lies another reason for traces of animosity that still exist against them. In 1861 King owned twenty thousand head of cattle and three thousand head of horses. With the eminent possibility of Civil War, he was determined not to give up what he had striven so long and hard to gain. He had a beloved wife and three baby children to create a future for.

With them in mind, he bent every effort to care for them and keep them safe.

At first, military demands drove horse and mule prices up, so the ranch was able to make a tidy sum on what they sold off. Cattle prices went in the opposite direction. Even though both North and South needed meat, Texas cattle were, as always, too far away from the markets. The threat of blockade was enough to keep cattle buyers away from the Boca del Rio, so prices sank to two dollars a head.

The only solution for many ranchers was to try to drive the herds to the closest deepwater port—New Orleans. Such expeditions were nightmares through marshes and mosquito-laden swamps where miserable cattle sometimes ran mad from the tormenting insects. Because of the horse sales, King held his herd for another year. Eventually he hoped to drive them into East Texas and cross the Mississippi at Vicksburg for delivery to Confederate forces.

Likely too were Mexican markets that opened up as U.S. markets closed and exports dropped to a trickle. Beef in Mexico in 1862 was selling for eleven dollars a head.

Another source of income for King was salt. A salt shortage in the Confederacy made extracting salt from *El Sal Viejo* and other saline lakes on the tidelands west of La Laguna Madre profitable. The residue had been left from seawater trapped in great shallow lakes when the Gulf of Mexico receded. Exposed for centuries to wind and boiling sun, washed from time to time by the infrequent rains, the crude mineral was nearly pure. It could be cut out in blocks and easily transported by mule teams.

Ever ready to seize every opportunity, King mined the mineral from the land unfit for anything else, the land nobody wanted, and sold it for profits that kept the ranch alive and going.

He was luckier too than the vast majority of Texas ranchers. In the southernmost tip of the Confederacy, the Santa Gertrudis lost few of her workers since his *Kineños* were Mexicans. Most ranchers in the rest of the state lost most of their cowboys. They had nobody to move their stock and, more importantly, nobody to defend them against depredations.

Texas had approximately 600,000 inhabitants. Sixty thousand Anglo-American men rode east to join the Confederacy and 27,000 more enlisted to defend the state. The population of the state was depleted by nearly fifteen percent.

Colonel Rip Ford recognized the problem immediately. Brazos de Santiago and the Port of Brownsville were indefensible against U.S. Navy guns. He enlisted Kenedy and King to use their steamboats to carry upriver the military stores abandoned by the army.

Meanwhile ranches in West Texas were under attack from other forces. The Comanches seized the opportunity to raid and steal almost at will. On May 19, 1861, Mexicans led by Cheno Cortinas attacked a fortified ranch across the river south of Zapata.

Fortunately, he had little time to entrench himself. He and his men were attacked by the Texas cavalry composed mostly of Texas-Mexican *rancheros* under the command of Captain Santos Benavides stationed at Rio Grande City. Benavides hit Cortinas like a thunderbolt, drove him back across the river, and did not stop there.

No longer hampered by U.S. laws and U.S. troops, he chased the bandit all the way to Guerrero in southern Tamaulipas. After that sound trouncing, Cortinas went into hiding to lick his wounds. Some thought they'd seen the end of him, but knowledgeable Texans knew that he was merely watching for another opportunity.

All along the Rio Grande there was little time or reason for celebrating Cortinas' rout. After the battle of Bull Run in July, a Union blockade was officially extended to the Texas coast. Wary eyes scanned the horizon, but no gun ships appeared.

For the time King and Kenedy's shipping enterprises were galvanized by the wartime economy with a real war actually in the offing. The planters of Texas had cotton aplenty to sell but no buyers unless they could transport it to Mexico. By January 1862 King could stand on his watchtower at the Santa Gertrudis and see the cotton wagons moving south down *his* road between *his* fenced pastures. Bound for Brownsville, they carried the hope of the Confederacy.

The mills of Europe—in Lancashire, Bremen, and Lyons—stood idle waiting for the cotton. Weavers, dyers, haberdashers, a whole host of guildsmen had no jobs. If gold was required to buy the cotton, gold the Confederacy would have. The whole world was feeling the pinch as the first real ramifications of global economy dawned.

The Matamoros market marked the beginning of the fabled wealth of *Los Algodones*, the cotton merchants, on the border. Richard King stood to profit in more ways than most in the Cotton Boom.

Wagonmasters, teamsters, and brokers' agents who stopped to camp by the Santa Gertrudis Creek came to the King's commissary to buy camp supplies as well as horses, mules, and beef for the last 125 miles. Ranch headquarters became the official receiving, storage, and shipping point for five-hundred-pound bales arriving from East Texas, Louisiana, Arkansas, and Missouri.

In some cases King wagons carried the cotton over the ranch to Brownsville for a transportation price. It was unloaded onto King wharves, which charged a rental fee.

From there the bales were lightered onto his riverboats, which charged ferrying services for transport to the vessels waiting offshore. Every step of the way Richard King made money.

Thirty-seven years old and in the prime of his life, he had no time to go to war. It had come to him.

February 15, 1862, the battle was joined—and swiftly—in the form of a Union man-of-war. Gulf watchers recognized the *Portsmouth* with her twenty-two guns the instant she hove in sight—a permanent blockader.

Kenedy & Co.'s new *Matamoros* was heading out from Boca del Rio with a full cargo for the English *Propeller* at anchor in the Gulf when the Union ship hove into view. The riverboat hastily churned back to Brownsville.

For nearly two weeks everywhere was consternation. Then Rip Ford called a *junta*. Kenedy, Stillman, Judge Trevino of Matamoros, the English consul, and several others attended this first of many Mexican councils of war.

King was on the Santa Gertrudis with Henrietta awaiting the birth of their fourth child. Alice was born on April 29, 1862. Her middle name was a memorial to the place that her mother, her sisters, and brother knew was home—Gertrudis.

The decisions that came from the meeting resulted in King's being able to continue his shipping business throughout the Civil War. Rip Ford made arrangements for M. Kenedy & Co. steamboats to fly the Mexican flag. At the same time, the English consul and the Mexican officials sent for the American captain of the *Portsmouth*, demanding to know whether he intended to blockade Mexico.

Of course, he had no orders to do so. He had no choice but to stand down while the *Matamoros* with the eagle and serpent flying from her masthead steamed out to transfer her goods. In her captain's breast pocket was a letter of mark listing her owner as a Mexican citizen.

By October 1862 Matamoros as well as most of north-eastern Mexico was booming. Millions of dollars' worth of munitions and medical supplies came through it in exchange for the cotton of the South. The North watched helplessly as vessels flying the Mexican flag sailed by them.

Because the rest of the South was effectively blockaded, cotton prices rose from sixteen cents a pound, to twenty-five. They were only beginning. In 1863 they were to rise as high as ninety cents. In 1865 they reached an all-time high of $1.25.

In 1863 the first glimpses of real war came to the Santa Gertrudis itself. A company of Confederate Texans passed through. They were reinforcements on their way to Ring-gold Barracks at Rio Grande City across the river from Camargo.

They camped beside the creek and came to the house requesting fresh meat. No one appeared to greet them. They were stalled by the *vaqueros*. The two cannon mounted in the top of the old blockhouse loomed menacingly.

Discouraged, they returned to their own camp. A short while later Captain King rode down to join them. He explained that he was satisfied that they were well disci-plined, so he fed them. The full weight of responsibility had settled on his shoulders. The safety of his family, his people, and lastly for the cotton the South depended on to pay for its supplies was his total concern.

Throughout 1863 across the prairie turned brown by a terrible drought, the tall cotton-wagons rolled. Twenty-mule teams pulled each one loaded with a dozen bales—six thousand pounds of cotton. The road from the Santa Ger-trudis to the Rio Grande was marked with tags of white fluff, just as the highways of the Valley are to this day during July and August. It dangled from every mesquite thorn, every Spanish dagger point, every clump of chaparral for a hundred and twenty-five miles.

And still thousands of bales were stored in plantation warehouses across East Texas and Louisiana with no way to transport them.

Richard King saw another opportunity to make money. He and his partners Kenedy and Stillman signed a contract with the Confederacy for a big operation that offered a big reward. It also made him a marked man. The Union would have his signature as proof of his activities.

A fiery rebel although he was born in New York City, he took over the task of delivering to the quartermaster at Brownsville five hundred bales of cotton per month for six months—$900,000 worth of cotton.

The further terms outlined were an advance of fifteen percent on the original cost and charges for the bales, plus a commission of two and a half percent for selling and two and a half percent for advancing. It was an incredibly lucrative contract that stood to make each partner $60,000 for six months' work.

The Confederacy had taxed each cotton grower one bale in ten. King was the man who rousted out those bales and hauled them south to the river. Kenedy met them at any point on the river where they could cross and ferried them down to Matamoros. Stillman sold them and moved them onto the decks of other steamboats flying the Mexican flag to foreign ships anchored at Boca del Rio.

Haste was the watchword. The three men knew the situation couldn't exist for very long. The North's strategy had been to starve the South into submission. If the Confederacy could plant and grow her own food and import her arms through the mouth of the Rio Grande, the war could go on indefinitely.

Abraham Lincoln did not have indefinitely. His term of office was more than half over. Since a blockade had not worked, the only solution was to mount a full-scale attack.

Bandits on the Border

All was not well in Mexico herself. The Civil War in America meant that the United States could no longer enforce the Monroe Doctrine. In 1862 the soldiers of Napoleon III of France landed at Veracruz ostensibly to collect debts Benito Juarez had ceased to pay when he was elected president of Mexico.

What Napoleon really wanted was control of Mexico through which he hoped to re-establish France's position on the North American continent. Although Juarez resisted, he was forced to flee Mexico City. With French troops holding their guns at the ready, Napoleon set up a monarchy and offered the crown of Mexico to Ferdinand Maximilian Hapsburg, an Archduke of Austria.

The situation throughout the country was perilously unstable. No one was really governing anything. Local fighting broke out in Matamoros where two rival factions, the *Rojos* and the *Crinolinos*, fought for control of Tamaulipas.

The situation imperiled the lifeline of the Confederacy. Of less importance in the grand scheme of things, but certainly of primary importance to King, Kenedy, and Stillman, was *Los Algodones* and the Cotton Boom.

The Confederate general on the Rio Grande was Hamilton Prioleau Bee, a nervous and ill-trained man. Under him were four companies of the Thirty-Third Texas Cavalry under Colonel James Duff, and the mounted militia of Captain Santos Benevidas stationed at Rio Grande City.

A renegade Texan, E. J. Davis, with a small band of guerrillas was stirring up trouble in Matamoros. The powder keg needed only a spark to explode into a conflagration. Who would it be?

Cheno Cortinas appeared suddenly as second in command to the military governor of Tamaulipas. A subordinate of his, Captain Adrian Vidal, even went so far as to attack Brownsville on October 28, 1863.

November 1 dawned on some of the worst luck in the history of Texas. Twenty-six transports carrying seven thousand Union troops nosed into the passage between Padre Island and Brazos de Santiago.

Fortunately for Bee, a storm was lashing the Gulf Coast. Heavy seas pounded four of the transport vessels until they sank. Landing boats capsized in the rolling surf. The half-drowned troops who managed to make the shore landed with their ammunition soaked. The efforts to land horses and artillery turned into a mêlée of cursing men, fighting whinnying animals, and rolling, shifting gun carriages tossed by battering winds and drenched by thundering waves.

As they struggled to land, all Brownsville knew they were coming. The town ran riot with rumors. A hundred well-led men could have turned the landing back into the sea. If Rip Ford had still been in command, it would have happened, but Bee was too frightened.

He ordered a retreat. Dumping his seige guns in the river, he ordered the installations and the cotton to be set afire. In the whipping wind, the blaze got out of hand within minutes. The orange glow dominated the skyline, and choking black smoke and ash filled the air. The citizens of Brownsville left it all to burn and sought to beat a panicky retreat to Matamoros.

The ferry was the only way across the river. There another mêlée ensued. Frightened people trying to escape with their household valuables pushed, shoved, and cursed. When eight thousand pounds of condemned gunpowder exploded with a great roar and mind-numbing concussion, they ran riot.

Firebrands shot high into the air and showered the town. The household goods the people had tried to carry away were consumed as they scattered back to their homes. Buildings along the waterfront caught fire, including M. Kenedy & Co. Fort Brown was destroyed. Two city blocks were badly burned.

For days the cotton on the levee continued to burn. A massive pall of black smoke billowed over the city.

South of the Rio Grande, Cheno Cortinas enjoyed his very personal triumph. Through skillful manuevering in the unsettled time, he had managed to become acting governor of Tamaulipas.

With a great deal of pleasure he summoned General N. J. T. Dana and turned the *Matamoros*, the *Mustang*, and the *James Hale*, the newest and best of the M. Kenedy & Co. fleet over to the Union. Grateful for the unexpected windfall, Dana put them to work immediately hauling his troops and supplies.

With the scratch of his pen and a smug smile, Cortinas had managed to place everything Richard King owned in jeopardy. At this point his steamboats were his security. Through them the economy of his shaky ranching operation, his cotton contracting affairs for the Confederacy, even his life were maintained. Now everything was in jeopardy.

Fortunately, King had already moved his family to the ranch including his father-in-law, Reverend Hiram Chamberlain, now sixty-six years old and ailing. When General Bee's army and supply train came past the Santa Gertrudis on November 8, King cursed him fervently.

Not only was Bee deserting his post without a fight, he had been intercepting and turning back King's wagon trains of cotton and even dumping and burning some of the bales to lighten and balance the loads so his men could retreat faster. Not satisfied with setting Brownsville ablaze, the incompetent coward now threatened to set the entire Wild Horse Desert ablaze.

The word of his actions was carried ahead of him and, to protect the cotton, the wagon bosses had taken to hiding the bales in the chaparral and in caches near the roadside. When the whole straggling band began to roll into the Santa Gertrudis, King's profanity matched theirs. He had a great deal to curse about. The half-empty cotton wagons kept on returning for several days.

Only Santos Benavides, who had been promoted to major and then again to colonel, held the river at Rio Grande City. The cotton routed in that direction continued to go through. Once on Mexican soil, it still moved efficiently through the Matamoros market to the foreign ships waiting in Boca del Rio.

In this manner the trade the Confederacy depended on so desperately did not cease altogether. Two factors kept it going. The river could be crossed at Rio Grande City, thanks to Santos Benavides. The cotton kept moving ever southward, and supplies, armaments, and ammunition kept moving northward, thanks to Richard King.

Frustrated at the sight of enemy trading going on the other side of a muddy river, the Union commander was determined to force Benavides's surrender and to capture King.

Despite his best efforts, Dana's entire force had managed to lay hands on only about eight hundred bales of cotton. By his own estimates twenty-five hundred had crossed the river at Rio Grande City within two weeks.

His orders were to keep it bottled up north of Laredo. In December he wrote the United States vice consul in Monterrey, "I desire to make the road from San Antonio to Eagle Pass and Laredo so perilous that neither Jew nor Gentile will wish to travel it. I wish to kill, burn, and destroy all that cannot be taken and secured."

Of course, his attention settled on the Santa Gertrudis and the man he called "a rebel agent," Richard King. How to get to him was a problem. James Richardson, whom his men called Santiago, King's foreman, had recruited a troop of 150 well-mounted and well-armed Texans. They, with the assistance of the *Kineños*, patrolled the Wild Horse Desert.

Three days before Christmas, a rider warned King that a troop of Yankees was coming to the ranch for the express purpose of arresting him. He might have resisted had his *Kineños* under the command of "Saint James" been at the ranch. Unfortunately, they were away on other business when King needed them most.

King made a terrible choice. He reasoned that resistance on his part would place them all in danger. Henrietta was seven months pregnant. The other children and their elderly grandfather would be imperiled by a headlong flight into the *brasada*. A blue norther could blow in sending the temperature plummeting thirty degrees in an hour and filling the air with ice crystals.

Surely women and children would not be molested if he left the ranch. He instructed them to offer no resistance and he sent for Francisco Alvarado, the *jefe* of the village in Tamaulipas. Alvarado had built many of the *Kineños' jacales* with his bare hands.

King ordered him to sleep in the house and take care of the family. Then Richard spoke to Henrietta and Reverend Chamberlain. He hugged and kissed his children and came out of the house with his black hat pulled down tight. His horse was ready, with guns on his saddle.

"You take care of my family," he said again to Alvarado.

"Si, Señor Capitán." Alvarado struck his breast.

Confident he had left his family in safe hands, King headed for Mexico where documents bearing his signature and the date have been found among government papers.

Henrietta must have felt as frightened as she could possibly feel with her Captain gone. Her prayers must have been more fervent and more frequent than at any other time in her young life. Richard was her foundation. If something should happen to him, if he should be arrested, tried, and shot as a spy, she would have lost everything.

She felt her child kick within her. She couldn't ride a bouncing stagecoach through the icy night. She couldn't put her children and her ailing father at such risk.

Two days passed and no one came. The guards on the watchtower reported no sightings.

Henrietta and her father talked and prayed about nothing else than the safety of them all and particularly Richard's safety. Within the walls of the ranch house, they felt as secure as anyone could be in these dangerous times. Hiram particularly placed great confidence in the gentlemanly qualities of U.S. Army officers. They would never intentionally harm civilians.

In the dawn of Christmas Eve, *La Patrona* roused to the thunder of horses' hooves. Yells and shots followed. A bullet slammed into the outside wall of the house. More shots followed. Then rifles boomed. Their larger charges of powder drove the lead through the walls and into the rooms. Glass broke. Henrietta raced to gather her frightened children.

Francisco Alvarado jumped to his feet. Unarmed, he threw open the door. The pale dawn light picked out his figure. He shouted, "Don't fire on the house! There is a family here—"

A ball smashed into his body dropping him dead in the doorway.

Union soldiers, their blue coats black with moisture in the dawn light, thudded across the porch. With cocked guns they entered the house. At the officer's command they picked up the dead man and carried him into the parlor in front of the fire.

Henrietta and her father came in with lighted lamps. Her face was white, but whether with fear or with righteous wrath, no one could tell. Her robe pulled tight over her gravid belly made every man among them look away after an embarrassed second.

Her heart pounded as she looked down at Francisco's bleeding body. She knew the command had been given to shoot because he had been mistaken for Richard King.

Her father, that good old man, was as angry as he had ever been in his life. His faith in the codes of chivalry and gallantry bled out with Francisco Alvarado's blood onto the living room floor.

Looking down into the *Kineño's* face, the Union officer saw a Mexican rather than the Anglo-American they wanted.

The soldiers heard the crying of children from the bedroom. The family of Francisco Alvarado, his wife and children, came in through the open door to bend over his body as the rising sun streamed through the broken windows.

To the weeping of women and children, the soldiers searched the house. They ran their sabers through the feather mattresses. They pulled the clothes out of the armoires and threw them on the floor.

Frustrated and guilty, their search turned into a rampage. They hadn't found the cotton agent. They determined to pillage his house. They smashed mirrors and china. They wrecked the fine furniture King had hauled in by oxcart to make a home for his wife. They stole his clothing and any of hers they thought they might give to some woman friend.

They rounded up all the horses and mules to drive back to Brownsville. All the adult males on the ranch—four Anglo-Americans and many *Kineños*—were herded into a prison pen.

A lieutenant came to take Hiram Chamberlain, who defied him. "You don't want me," he said. "I am an old man of sixty-seven and a minister of the gospel."

Then word came that riders were in the area. Could it be a Confederate force? Or worse, a troop of Texas Rangers? The soldiers had heard rumors of *los diablos Tejanos*. They left the ranch on Christmas Eve as hastily as they had come. For fear of retaliation they didn't shoot any of the men in the prison pen.

Although they'd been sent to capture cotton and bring it back to Brownsville, they left it behind. Hundreds of five-hundred-pound bales would slow them down. They greatly feared that the consequences of what they had done would catch up with them.

𝓌 𝓌 𝓌

On February 22, 1864, in San Patricio beyond the Nueces, Henrietta Chamberlain King gave birth to a healthy, strong baby boy. Her mouth set in a thin line, she pronounced her defiance to the Yankees and the world. She named her new son Robert E. Lee King.

As soon as she was able, she moved her family to San Antonio out of harm's way.

𝓌 𝓌 𝓌

Her Captain did his level best to sustain the Confederacy. He—who hated to ride—rode every day back and forth across the Wild Horse Desert. He kept the cotton wagons moving past the Yankee patrols. Along with the cotton he delivered beef and supplies. Once they were through, he ran supplies back across. As often as he could, he rode to the Santa Gertrudis to lead his men to protect it from rustlers who stole his cattle and horses.

In these terrible months, he and every other rancher in Texas received a gift from the weather. To this day it is remembered as the "Big Drift." In January a succession of northers came blowing down off the Great Plains. Galveston Bay froze over. Port Isabel was almost iced in. The northern ranges west of the Mississippi were not yet fenced, and the cattle from Iowa, Nebraska, Kansas, Colorado, and Wyoming came drifting down by the tens of thousands to escape the killing cold. They ended up on the shores of the Gulf of Mexico.

Because of the war, owners could not claim their stock. The drifting herds increased and multiplied the numbers of cattle on the South Texas ranges, especially on the Santa Gertrudis.

As Hiram Chamberlain might have said, "The Lord giveth and the Lord taketh away."

The loss of so many good men during the war was a terrible price to pay for a few head of cattle.

A Deafening Silence

In the last days of the Confederacy, Richard King served for a while as a private soldier in "Santiago" Richardson's company. His cotton contract had long run out, but he kept his wagons rolling.

Until the Union forces came in earnest, M. Kenedy & Co. was going to make every effort to get all the cotton into the hands of cotton agents. With the North sure the Confederacy could last no more than a matter of days, the blockade was unofficially removed. Speculators frantically sought to make a profit on their investments before the South could grow another crop.

Plenty of money was to be made. While the rest of the South was circulating now worthless Confederate dollars, the southern tip of Texas was tied to the hard currency of Mexico. For the first time in a long time, Texas found she needed to aid revolution-torn Mexico.

ꟽ ꟽ ꟽ

King's other reason to keep the wagons moving was to bring supplies to his friend Rip Ford in San Antonio. The colonel had organized a troop to fight for Texas now that the majority of the Confederate troops had been withdrawn, leaving the state all but defenseless.

Ford called his men the Cavalry of the West. With ever-changing numbers, they had no more than a thousand men and boys at any one time. One of Ford's officers complained, "Fifty-seven children have joined my battalion."

The cavalry mounted in front of the Alamo. They were ill clothed in all shades of gray and butternut. Some wore *sombreros*. Ford mounted at its head in his black hat with a sword sash around his lean waist. They sang "The Yellow Rose of Texas."

To look at them, no West Point trained military man would have thought they were dangerous.

He would have been wrong.

ᴡ ᴡ ᴡ

In March 1865 the ranking Union and Confederate officers still on the Rio Grande met at Brazos de Santiago. Since the war was all but over, they reasoned that more bloodshed would not serve any purpose. Between themselves they effected an uneasy truce.

On April 9, 1865, Robert E. Lee surrendered at Appomattox Court House hundreds of miles from Texas and the nebulous peace that hung in the air there like a thin mist.

In May 1865 Ford led his troop down to Brownsville, his eye on the Yankees for any sign that the truce would be violated. On the twelfth he dined with his superior, Brigadier General James Slaughter, a man ill suited to be a warrior. Slaughter had received a dispatch that sixteen hundred Union troops were moving on Brownsville.

They were to be the beginning of reprisals. The plan was for the Union to occupy the town so they could impose their own sort of rapacious peace on all of South Texas.

"General," Ford asked, "what do you intend to do?"

"Retreat," Slaughter replied.

"You can retreat and go to Hell if you wish. These men are mine, and I am going to fight!" Ford declared.

The next day, May 13, he led his men out into a thick clump of brush that curved along the edge of Palo Alto plain where the Indiana and New York regiments rested, dead tired from the oppressive heat and humidity.

Mounted on a nervous, prancing horse, Ford shouted at his Texans, "Men, we have whipped the enemy in all previous fights. We can do it again."

His troops cheered.

The Union soldiers heard the noise and fired into the thicket.

Over their salvo Ford yelled, "Charge!"

Three hundred horsemen yelled so loudly their shrieking could be heard above the guns three miles over the prairie. Like a tidal wave they burst out of the palmettos and mesquites and struck the Union flank. Nothing on earth could have stopped them.

The veteran Union troops broke and ran. Those who tried to stand and fight were run down to the last man as the cavalry thundered onward. For seven miles Ford's men chased the fleeing troops. They did not stop until their horses were kneedeep in the waves at Brazos de Santiago.

When Ford withdrew and took his count, he had not lost a single man. The 34th Indiana had lost more than two-thirds of its troops. One hundred and eleven enlisted men and four officers had been taken prisoner.

*

The last battle of the Civil War, fought when the war was over, had been a terrible victory. Just as the war had been a terrible war.

After Palmito Hill there was no formal surrender of Confederate forces. The Confederate government simply melted away. Rip Ford had left no one to surrender to, and the Union had lost its stomach for force against *los diablos Tejanos* until the war was officially over.

General Slaughter, who was nominally Ford's superior officer, tried to seize an opportunity for himself. He sold the Confederate artillery to General Mejía, the Imperialist officer in Matamoros, for twenty thousand silver pesos. He planned to accompany the artillery to Mexico and keep the money for himself.

Ford arrested him at pistol point and forced Slaughter to sign over his command and dismiss his men. Ford then used the silver to pay his own men, who had fought the last battle with him.

He kept four thousand for himself, but he was still deeply in debt. He had outfitted much of the cavalry out of his own pockets. On May 26 Ford took his family across the river and placed them under Mejía's protection. Then he went back to face the oncoming Union troops.

Some diehards from the Cavalry of the West were joined by Confederates from Arkansas and Louisiana, even as far away as Missouri. They mounted for the last time and rode south to join Maximilian's beleaguered army. At the Rio Grande they wrapped their Southern battle standards in canvas and buried them in the sand. There they rotted unresurrected.

ʬ ʬ ʬ

Although the battle of Palmito Hill gave M. Kenedy & Co. another two weeks to sell their cotton, so far as the war was concerned, it was a Pyrrhic victory.

A Union force 25,000 strong under the command of Major General Philip Henry Sheridan arrived. They were sent by command of Ulysses S. Grant for the express purpose of punishing Texas. A strong force marched into Brownsville on May 30.

They were too late. Slaughter had sold the Confederate arms and ammunition. The Cavalry of the West had already disbanded. The Confederates still in uniform had crossed into Mexico.

Sheridan was furious. He called it a "swindle." The rebels had plundered the rightful spoils of the U.S. Army. He sent representatives to Imperialist General Tomas Mejía demanding the return of the Confederate supplies. The general did not even acknowledge the letter.

Sheridan's wrath made the war seem a pleasant dream compared to the Reconstruction peace. Rebels hated Yankees. French Imperialists loyal to Emperor Maximilian hated the *Juaristas*. White men hated the Negro Union troops whom Sheridan had brought to put over them.

And in the language of the border "gringos" hated "greasers."

ꟿ ꟿ ꟿ

In the summer of 1865 Major General Frederick Steele commanded the Union occupation forces at Brownsville. He sent for Ford. Old Rip came flanked by his friends and co-conspirators—Mifflin Kenedy, Richard King, and others who had maintained the stability of the region.

Steele was as gracious in victory as his former enemies were in defeat. Looking into the eyes of eagles, he saw that nothing would be served by persecuting these prominent and powerful men. In fact, he would do a disservice to himself, the Union, and all of Texas if he sought to punish them.

Therefore, he parolled them.

They in return promised to answer his call for anything and everything they could provide in the ways of both services and goods. One of the first services was for M. Kenedy & Co. to recommission the steamboats under American flags and resume business as usual.

The Amnesty Proclamation of the President of the United States required a former Confederate to take an oath to support and defend the Constitution of the United States. Certain classes of Confederates, such as those who had held high offices in the government and those who owned taxable property valued at more than twenty thousand dollars, were declared ineligible to take the oath.

King was a targeted member of that class. His name had appeared frequently in dispatches sent to Washington, and his notoriety had been brought to the attention of more than one Union officer. The situation for him was going to be extremely difficult.

He had seen his wife very little during the last years. After Lee's birth in February of 1864, she had moved the children to San Antonio. Whether he was ever with her during those last eighteen months is unknown. His work for the Confederacy kept him constantly on the move across the Wild Horse Desert with little chance to ride another hundred miles north.

He wanted to bring his wife and children to live with him in Brownsville. Lee and Alice scarcely knew him. He had missed much of the childhood of Henrietta, Ella, and Richard. He could not return to his beloved Santa Gertrudis. Under parole, he was obliged to live and work in Brownsville according to his agreement with General Steele.

~ ~ ~

On September 15 he applied for possession of his house on Elizabeth Street. It had been occupied only occasionally for the past three years and was then occupied by a military tenant since June. He feared that it would need extensive repairs before his family could occupy it. Nevertheless, he was eager to bring them to his side. In the application he tells that he is anxious to resume his "residence in Brownsville, as a citizen of the United States."

The interesting thing is that the residency was granted as well as his citizenship shortly thereafter. In a time when former Confederate heroes had to humiliate themselves, when they were stripped of nearly everything they owned by the military commandant Phil Sheridan and later by the carpetbagger governor E. J. Davis, Richard King had his citizenship reinstated with hardly a murmur.

The reason lay with Rip Ford. His gallantry and good sense was highly respected by the Union. Generally, they did what he said. In this case, he is believed to have interceded for his friend.

His intercession was something that Richard King never forgot.

The Myth

The Lost Gold of the Confederacy

The lieutenant led his troop at a gallop out of Brownsville. Instead of his uniform, he wore a black duster over a dark suit. His sergeant and his six troopers also were dressed in civilian clothes. Leading six pack mules, each piled high with supplies, they quickly left the lights of the border behind.

The plan was that they would pass as merchants on their way north should anybody ask. If they were discovered by Union troops, they might be shot as spies.

Out of sight of prying eyes, they left the muddy road that led north towards the Wild Horse Desert to head east and pick their way through the salt marshes along the Laguna Madre.

It was the safest way to travel, the lieutenant reasoned. The vegetation then was not the tangle of mesquite, huisache, and cactus that today is called the *brasada*. It had not yet spread like a cancer across the sea of grass. In the marshes, the grass was quite low. Even though the ground was soggy and the mosquitos made the night hell, he believed his troop could make good time.

They had little time. The Confederacy was dying, starving behind the Union blockade. It had no gold to buy food or ammunition. Word had come that the Union ships were offshore at Boca del Rio. The Union force was about to land.

A considerable sum of gold from the coffers of Southern sympathizers on both sides of the Rio Grande rested in small strongboxes beneath tarpaulins, blankets, and miscellaneous bivouac supplies on the backs of these mules.

There was a chance, a slim one, that a few good men might slip away, ride at night around the bend of the Gulf coastal plain, and take a small boat across the Sabine. From there they might make their way north to Nachitoches and on east into the heart of the Confederacy with gold to ease the inevitable suffering when the war ground to its end.

The lieutenant had been chosen to lead this expedition because he was young and brave. Moreover, he was idealistic and Puritanically honest. He lived for honor and glory. He would never be tempted to steal the last gold of the South.

Through the night they rode. Once off the road, their pace slowed as they themselves walked to rest their horses. The sergeant was sent out ahead to reconnoiter. He led them over a crest of walking hills, sand dunes blown inland by hurricane winds. By morning the troop was gazing at the gray-green waters of the Laguna Madre. It lapped along the edge of a broad mud flat, striped white with brine that marked high tide.

The lieutenant smiled when he saw the broad flat surface extending northward. They could travel swiftly now. This journey would be almost too easy.

He called a halt. The men slid gratefully from their horses. The ground was damp, but they spread their slickers and instantly fell asleep as the day brightened and the temperature rose.

In the late afternoon they moved out onto the mud flat. To their shock, they found the going harder than they had expected. The heavily laden pack mules broke through the mud crust. The struggles of the poor animals to get out left them exhausted and the men who had to tug and shove them no less so.

The lieutenant was wild with frustration. He had pictured thankful people greeting him, hailing him as a savior.

Now they had no choice but to get off the flat. If a mule were injured, the whole expedition would be in jeopardy. Gold was heavy. To load another with its share would lead to its injury, and so on, and so on. Failure was a dismal prospect.

They left the flat to jog over the sea grape vines and short, sparse grass on the edge of the dunes. With every rise of an iron shod hoof, saltwater rose in its track. Atop a dune, the lieutenant looked back over his shoulder. He frowned and whistled through his bared teeth. A blind man could read their trail. The spots where the mules had floundered looked like great holes left by cannonballs on a battlefield.

He looked north. Everything was the same: the Gulf on the left, the *brasada* on the right, and the mud flats, dunes, and salt marshes in between.

Before they had gone a mile, another problem beset them. They came to the bank of a narrow *resaca*. The horses dipped their heads to drink in the green water, then backed away in disgust. The mules, being smarter, did not even wet their lips.

The lieutenant had not reckoned with the total absence of fresh water. Still, he reasoned it could not be too far ahead. He ordered his sergeant and a trooper to ride both north and northwest. He would lead a mule and continue along the route. Whoever found water first would return and lead the others to it.

The sergeant came back the next day with the news that for a day's ride nothing was fresh. The trooper never came back.

The lieutenant cursed the man for having deserted, but the sergeant cocked an eye up to the rising moon. "He might've been captured, sir. Or killed."

They pressed on. The horses' heads hung low. The troopers slouched in their saddles. The mules plodded bravely on, but they too were flagging.

Suddenly out of nowhere a fierce yelling began. Screaming their *gritas*, Mexican *bandidos* descended on the badly outnumbered soldiers. The fight was hot but short—a volley of shots almost drowned out by screaming, cursing men fighting for their lives.

The *bandidos* managed to cut loose one mule. With it in tow, they rode away as swiftly as they had come.

When the smoke had cleared, the lieutenant counted his losses. Two troopers had toppled dead from their saddles. Another was badly wounded. A downed horse whinnied in pain from a shattered shoulder.

Of the eight men who had begun the mission, only five remained and one was unable to ride. Two animals had been lost.

"Give it up, sir," the sergeant advised.

"No. Our duty—"

"Duty! Hell! At the rate we're a-goin' there won't be no Confederacy to deliver this to."

The lieutenant said nothing. He thrust out his chin.

The sergeant cocked his head to one side. "What you think's gonna happen when those Mexicans unload that mule and find the gold?"

The lieutenant closed his eyes. "We'll have to travel faster."

"I was afraid you'd say that." The sergeant had already pulled his pistol from his belt and leveled it at the officer. "Get off that horse, shavetail."

The lieutenant didn't say a word. Without a change of expression, he slid off his horse. In one smooth motion he drew his service revolver and shot the sergeant from under his mount's neck.

The remaining two troopers stared at the bodies around them, then exchanged quick glances. Dropping the mules' lead ropes, they spurred away, galloping back toward Brownsville as fast as they could travel.

The lieutenant dared not follow to try to bring them back. Even though others deserted, he could not do so. He tied the mules together in a string. He caught the sergeant's horse and led it to the side of his last surviving trooper, but the man was unconscious. Even as the officer tried to hold a canteen to his lips, he died.

The lieutenant looked around him desperately. He knew only duty. The Confederacy must have the gold. He mounted and headed north.

For two days he traveled, without water, until he became disoriented and, finally, lost. Beside another brackish *resaca*, he slid out of the saddle. He had no choice but to bury the gold, turn the mules loose, and ride as fast as he could north to fresh water. He knew he would be welcome on the King Ranch. There he could get fresh horses and some *Kineños* to help him carry out his mission.

But his pace was too swift. His mind was too hazy from his own thirst to set a proper one. He came out of the salt grass onto the mud flat. Before he realized where he was, his horse had broken through the crust. Its leg slid into the mire. Its shoulder snapped.

With a terrible scream, the animal crashed headlong. The lieutenant went flying. Face first, he struck the mud. He heard a snapping sound. His last thought was that he felt no pain.

He knew he was dead. He stared down at his body, face down in the mud, his head all but buried. The horse too was dead. He looked around.

Where was Heaven?

The light seemed brightest in the east. He looked longingly at the water and the crystal clearness beyond.

He couldn't go there until he completed his mission. The gold. The gold for the Confederacy. He must find someone to tell, someone who would take the gold for him.

ᴡ ᴡ ᴡ

The *Kineños* tell the stories to this day.

"A ghost accompanied me to the next ranch many times, step by step," an old man said.

He and other ranch workers reported seeing a man dressed in black. His face was indistinct in the semidarkness. He would appear and disappear by the water tower at Norias. Sometimes he seemed to try to come toward them, but his image would fade before their eyes. Many times he would motion for them to come to him.

They never would.

"Yes, there are ghosts," another old man said. "A man dressed in black has appeared on the way to my father-in-law's house many times. He walked beside me all the way."

The thought that a ghost was actually appearing close to the *colonía* bothered him a great deal.

In the early morning hours, *Kineños* out at the cow camps during the roundups have reported seeing fires. These were very troublesome because the *vaqueros* had to ride out to investigate. When they got to the spots where they thought the fires must have been, they would find nothing. No ashes, no embers—nothing at all.

One man saw a fire three or four feet high. He rode to it and found the ground blackened, but there were no ashes. The spot looked as if a fire had been built there a long time ago.

To this day the lieutenant cannot take his rest. Still he signals desperately for someone to come and take the gold to the South.

Part IV

A Bloody Peace

The Truth

R. King & Co.

The Union occupation had confiscated many of King's steamboats in defiance of their Mexican registry. M. Kenedy & Co. was technically without vessels even though it still operated them and General Steele had made use of them.

Both King and Kenedy knew that a great deal of work lay ahead of them if they were to get their company up and running again. Moreover, James Walworth, one of their partners, had died in April 1865. His widow had to be paid $50,000 by M. Kenedy & Co. It was no less than she was entitled to, but it constituted a big financial slice out of working capital at a time when cash money was desperately needed.

Charles Stillman wanted to settle his affairs in Matamoros and move back to New York. Though younger than King he was in failing health. He correctly foresaw that he wouldn't be able to fight the political and economic battles of the next decade. Of all people, Kenedy and King knew they would miss "Don Carlos" the most. As well as his canny business sense for making money, he took another very large chunk of their capital. In fact, he took enough money out of Mexico and Texas to develop the National City Bank of New York.

With their two partners gone, the process of refitting the steamboat company to a profitable postwar operation was a daunting task. The steamboats *Matamoros*, *Mustang*, and *James Hale*, which had been new at the beginning of the war were old and decrepit now. In fact, they were scarcely worth reacquiring from the U.S. Army. Evidently the quartermaster thought so too, because the department was now ready to get rid of them.

New boats had to be bought with the idea that they could provide quick infusion of capital. For the first time in four years, Kenedy went back to Pittsburgh. He returned with the *Antonio*, *Eugenia*, *Tamaulipas*, and the *Camargo*. Rather than putting these vessels into their service immediately, the company turned a quick profit. The *Tamaulipas* was chartered to the United States Quartermaster. The *Antonio* and *Eugenia* were sold to the Imperialist forces holding Matamoros.

Only the *Camargo* was actually put into use by King and Kenedy. During the next four years they acquired and sold other vessels, but they kept their records purposely incomplete. In this way they thwarted Union inventories and taxes.

In 1866 at age forty-two, Richard King began to ease himself out of the steamboat business. Even though it had been his first love and the source of his first fortune, he realized that it would never be the business it had been before and during the war. Although he joined with his partner in trying to sustain their freight hauling monopoly on the Rio Grande, he must have known they had little hope of doing so.

When Henrietta's father, Hiram Chamberlain, died November 1, a strong reason to stay in Brownsville died with him. Henrietta's stepmother wanted to take their youngest child and move back East to live. Henrietta's four half brothers, of course, wanted to stay with the Kings.

Richard welcomed them with open arms. The Santa Gertrudis would be a good place to raise boys. The number of his children grew from five to nine. When he had to be away from them on business trips, he wrote letters to Henrietta wanting to know how all his "Pets" were getting along.

At the same time he began dreaming a new dream—a new mode of transportation that would tie the United States together as boats had never been able to do. A railroad stretching from Chicago to the Santa Gertrudis would take his cattle to market faster and more efficiently than anything yet seen. It could realize his dream of selling not just hides and tallow but meat.

He recognized cattle as the way for Texas to survive the injustices of Reconstruction. A standing steer in Texas was worth twice or three times as much in the Midwest if a man could get it there.

The bustling stockyards and meatpacking plants in Chicago, St. Louis, and Kansas City were evidence of a new industry springing up. The new urban worker lived on paved streets with sidewalks completely covering the land in front of and between the buildings. He needed and wanted beef. Indeed, he needed all the foods he ate. Although he could no longer raise them for himself, he could buy them with his wages earned.

America was waiting for the Texas trail drive to the railroad and thence to the packing plant.

* * *

With these theories and dreams in his mind, the future must, nevertheless, have seemed very, very far away to King in 1867. In June Emperor Maximilian was betrayed by his own trusted aide. The troops of Benito Juarez executed him by firing squad against a wall in Querétaro. As he fell, the Imperialists who held sway in Matamoros fell with him.

Suddenly, the Confederates had nowhere to run. Trade advantages had made them allies with the French cause. Now they were up against the Rio Grande with Union forces on one side and *Juaristas* on the other.

In September 1867 the lower Rio Grande suffered a major disaster. A hurricane roared in from the Gulf and ripped through both Brownsville and Matamoros, causing untold damage and loss of life. It knocked most of the buildings flat at Brazos de Santiago and destroyed the military railroad. It destroyed the M. Kenedy & Co. steamboat terminal at the White Ranch and sank four of their steamers.

Fortuitously, King had already moved his family back to the Santa Gertrudis, which now totaled more than 146,000 acres. The number of head of livestock is unknown. The depredations of the Civil War and the subsequent rustling during Reconstruction played havoc with the records.

In November 1867 Kenedy too decided that he wanted to go back to ranching. He had sold his land close to Rio Grande City rather than let it be overrun during the war. His cattle were mixed in with King's. From Charles Stillman's brother, he acquired twenty-six leagues of land on the Laureles grant, directly east of the Santa Gertrudis.

Mindful of all the advantages that King had carved out for himself and his family in its proximity to Corpus Christi, he concluded that he wanted to take his wife and family there. King and he drew up a partnership agreement to divide the cattle. The strength of their friendship and the respect in which they held each other is testified to in the method by which they finally divided their goods.

On May 31, 1868, the partners signed an instrument entitled "Articles of Agreement and Settlement Between R.

King and M. Kenedy." By its terms all the livestock—cattle, horses, mules, donkeys, sheep, and goats—were divided two at a time so that each man had as far as possible an exactly equal share in value.

As a result of the "Big Drift" in the winter of 1863-64, each man ended up with many more head of cattle than he had imagined. That they were other men's cattle troubled them not at all. They had eaten Santa Gertrudis grass for five years.

Kenedy recorded that he stopped accepting cattle when he had twenty-five thousand head. King branded 23,664 head. He estimated another ten thousand to be on the prairie. Additionally, the friends divided 4,400 head of horse stock.

At the time of this division, King began to brand his stock with the new brand he had chosen because of its practicality. It could be placed on a steer's hide with a running iron just as easily as with a stamp. It had no corners where infection might set in. It was difficult if not impossible to blot. The *Kineños* called it the *viborita* or little snake. The world came to know it as the Running W.

That same year, the spring of 1870, King began the first of his great cattle drives to the railhead at Abilene, Kansas. The Texas drovers already knew the way. Eleven hundred miles lay between Santa Gertrudis headquarters and the cattle pens alongside the Kansas Pacific.

Yet could any animal that must graze and drink survive ten to twelve miles a day for a hundred days? King's half-wild longhorns were ideally constituted for the walk. They were tough enough to survive anything.

From the Santa Gertrudis they strung out north through Austin, Waco, and Fort Worth. Along the way they had to cross nearly twenty rivers great and small that drained off the Balcones into the Gulf of Mexico. Nearly five hundred miles along the way, they crossed the treacherous Red with its sinkholes and quicksand, the first of many rivers that drained into the Mississippi. Through the Oklahoma Territory they made their way over the famous Chisholm Trail to Caldwell, to Wichita, and finally to the railhead at Abilene, Kansas.

Most of the cattle arrived in good condition. A steer worth eleven dollars in Texas brought twenty gold dollars from a buyer in Abilene, who sold it in the Chicago stockyards for $31.50. In three trail drives in three successive years, King sold 13,500 head of beef.

With that kind of money financing them, King and Kenedy immediately began to fence off more of their land. Kenedy's land was bounded on three sides by water. Still he had to build thirty miles of fence made of creosoted cypress posts and pine planks to enclose his 131,000 acres. It became the first fenced range of any size west of the Mississippi.

Because the Santa Gertrudis had no natural borders, King had to be satisfied with enclosing merely the tract around the ranch headquarters. At the same time he branded fifty thousand head of cattle.

On September 21, 1870, another document entitled "Agreement and Final Settlement of Affairs of R. King & Co." was filed in the Nueces County Courthouse. The King-Kenedy partnership that had begun March 1, 1850, was formally dissolved.

For twenty years the men had worked together. Now they were formally going to part, but their friendship and loyalty never faded. Decades later, Mifflin Kenedy would tell a grandson of Richard King, "Your grandfather and I had lots of fights. Always on the same side."

ꟺ ꟺ ꟺ

To the *Kineños* as well as the Mexicans who raided the Santa Gertrudis in the years following the war, the *viborita* or little snake, meant something else. *Cuidadito*!, the Spanish word for "Be very careful!" attached itself to the symbol. The ancient serpent image is on the Mexican flag. Beware, danger, retribution, "don't tread on me" are all implied in the single brand.

Whether King thought of all those things when he chose it, or where it came from, is unknown. Certainly, when he learned how the Mexicans regarded it, he took full advantage of its power.

~ ~ ~

Apart from King's first successful cattle drive, 1870 was a terrible year for the majority of the citizens of Texas. E. J. Davis was elected governor in the most perverted election in the state's history. Davis was a renegade and scalawag pretending to be a Republican. He was guilty of criminal activity in Matamoros during the war. Now he became the governor of Texas for a four-year term.

Perhaps in retaliation for the "escapes" of many prominent Confederates and many thousands of dollars' worth of materiel into Mexico, General Philip Sheridan turned over the reins of the military government to Davis after hearing the man declare loudly that the state could not hold another election of any kind until 1872 when it had been properly "reconstructed."

Sheridan also knew how the election of 1870 had been conducted. Polling had been a farce. More than half the white men in the state still had not regained their citizenship. In East Texas the Negros had been marched from their cabins on the plantations where they still lived, lined up at the polling places, and instructed where to make their marks. The Democrats put up a candidate although they knew he couldn't win. Disgust and disillusionment were everywhere as the state braced for what they were sure would come.

Their wildest nightmares would not have prepared them for what Davis and his men wrought. Ostensibly to replace the Texas Rangers, who had been disbanded by Sheridan, a state police was created under the command of the governor with the unconstitutional privileges of taking offenders from one county to another for trial and of operating as secret agents. The Militia Bill put all males in Texas under the command of the governor, who had the right to suspend civil law, to declare martial law in any county in Texas, and to maintain that law indefinitely.

The Enabling Act provided that the governor should appoint all hitherto elected officials all over Texas. The Printing Bill provided for an official public printer that would send newspapers throughout the state the news they were supposed to print. No other state in the Union was subjected to such conditions, nor have such conditions been imposed elsewhere in the entire history of the United States.

Firmly in control of everything civil, Davis cast his avaricious sights on the cotton plantations of Texas. They were a natural target since they employed what the Civil War was ostensibly all about—slaves. Also cotton had been king. At the end of the war the prices were high. What hadn't slipped past the blockade or run through the Santa Gertrudis had been stored in warehouses and barns all over the Trans-Mississippi South.

For four years Davis held sway while the price of cotton fell to thirteen cents a pound. The small farms were wiped out first, then the great plantations.

The planter's market was glutted, his paper money was fit only for kindling, his slaves and capital had vanished, his taxes were past due. So far as he was concerned his land was worthless.

Mortgage sales were universal. Virtually all the land in East Texas passed into the hands of other owners. Because of the nature of their antebellum lives, the planters had no skills and no resilience to withstand humiliation. They completely and utterly disappeared.

And E. J. Davis took his share of every transaction, every dirty acre, every bale, every gracious home, every small farm. All across the South, the culture of King Cotton passed into history.

𝔚 𝔚 𝔚

Though the name of Richard King was known throughout the state, though he owned more land than probably any other person, and though he had a past history of dealings with Davis, King was not a prime target. Again the ranch itself, the Wild Horse Desert, *El Desierto de los Muertos*, the land nobody wanted, saved its owner from persecution. The Santa Gertrudis was too harsh, demanded too much, had too little that could be stripped away. Its wealth ran deep—its vast prairies of grass, its cattle, its free-flowing creeks, all that was intrinsic to it.

The scalawags and carpetbaggers had little interest in it. Besides the word was that King was losing hundreds of head of cattle every year to rustlers. Without the Texas Rangers, with no local law enforcement, he couldn't sustain those losses. The bandits would overrun him.

When King was wiped out financially, they said, his land could be picked up without any trouble.

The question was whether anybody wanted to take the trouble.

"Los Gringos Crian Las Vacas Por Mi."

The joke among every itinerant *vaquero*, every *bandido*, every *ranchero* along the Rio Grande was, "The *gringos* are raising cows for me." On the spur of the moment, any man could make a ride across the river to pick up a few head and sell them anywhere in Tamaulipas for three or four dollars. They'd spent nothing but their effort.

If anyone questioned their honesty, they rationalized their thievery by saying that the border of Mexico was really the Nueces River anyway. The Texans, *los diablos Tejanos*, had stolen it. Therefore, the cattle and horses raised on it by right belonged to them. With conditions so unsettled in Mexico, no one cared that stolen cattle were coming across the river. On the contrary, the rustlers' enterprise was applauded.

The most profitable rancher within reach of their *riatas* was Richard King. Such a flood of rustlers raided his land that his *Kineños* were significantly outnumbered. One estimate puts the number of cattle King lost over the four years of Davis's administration at well over fifty thousand head.

King estimated that to fence in his entire ranch would probably cost him fifty thousand dollars, but he would make his money back in a year. With an eye to controlling and eventually eliminating all invasions of his kingdom, he designed fences with guard stations at regular intervals. He bought thirty stands of Henry rifles and a supply of ammunition. He hired riders to take commands from Santiago Richardson, whose main job as foreman of the Santa Gertrudis was waging a war against rustlers.

The rustlers sought to retaliate. They were no longer after only his cattle. He became their target. His banks and places of business were still in large part in Brownsville. He had to carry large amounts of money, sometimes as much as fifty thousand dollars, to and from them. To travel there was like riding into the lion's mouth.

To ensure that he wouldn't be robbed, he made elaborate preparations. His stagecoach was outfitted with a steel strongbox. Only he, his ranch manager Reuben Holbein, and his wife knew that it existed. If others had known or even suspected, the *bandidos* would have lined up the entire length of the ranch to capture the coach.

As always Henrietta was his dearest partner and confidant, as well as his "Pet" and the mother of all his other "Pets." Her courage and fortitude were truly remarkable. Every time he started out, she lived with knowledge that he might never come back. Therefore, rather than know nothing about his business as most wives of her time, she knew everything. He told her everything, knowing that he might never come back. She might have to take the reins of the Santa Gertrudis into her hands.

Unlike many husbands of his time, he trusted her to do so.

Outriders rode before and after, as well as patrolling his flanks. For each trip King kept their names in his account books as well as the money he paid them. For years men with names like Mantavo, Villanueva, Flores—*Kineños* all—put their lives in jeopardy for *El Señor Capitán*. His books also listed $7.50 worth of whiskey as supplies for the men, and he shared it with them all along the way. He set up stage camps at twenty-mile intervals along the Brownsville road with fresh horses and mules. He traveled fast. His life depended on it.

On one occasion, he gave a ride to another man. Six miles from the ranch house at San Fernando Creek at eight o'clock in the evening, his party was ambushed. A volley of shots was fired directly into the coach. His passenger died from a bullet through the head. Thinking they'd killed King, the shooters ceased fire and simply melted back into the brush. Neither driver, guard, nor outriders were touched.

The ambush was clearly an assassination attempt.

If they had come near the coach, they would have learned King's weapon of choice was a double-barreled shotgun loaded with buckshot. It was sheathed in a hand-tooled leather scabbard strapped inside the coach. No one doubted that he would use it.

King was a man in whom the struggle to survive had been refined into the art of living. He never questioned his life, never thought about selling out and going back to New York as Stillman had done. He had bought land. He owned cattle and horses. He had a wonderful wife, five glorious children, and four handsome nephews. Whatever he had to do to maintain them was his life.

To this end he began to buy more land. As ranchers around him went under, he bought them out with the capital from his cattle drives. He remembered El Sauz, the dry *rancho* that Legs Lewis had led him past that long ago day. Part of the *San Juan Carricitos* grant, it was covered with some of the best grass in the Wild Horse Desert. With wells dug on it, it would become some of his best land. Till the time of his death he struggled to discover all the heirs and prove up all the titles. Land became an obsession with him. He never stopped buying it.

He observed that heavier, softer cattle drew better prices than longhorns at the railheads. In 1873 he took his family north to Kentucky to put Nettie and Ella in a fine finishing school.

During that trip he bought a hundred head of especially fine Durham cattle with the idea of crossing them with longhorns and improving his herd. He had already done much work in improving his horses, which were accounted some of the best in Texas. Now he began the task of improving his cattle, a task that he never completed. Even on the King Ranch in the present day, improving the cattle is of primary importance.

ꟽ ꟽ ꟽ

From 1871 through 1878, the thieves were aided and abetted in their practices by the new brigadier general of the Mexican army, commander of the line of the Bravo, the name the Rio Grande bears on its southern bank. Cheno Cortinas had returned as a *Juarista*. His ability to keep his feet upon the shifting sands of Mexican politics was now fabled. Through the regimes of Santa Anna, of Juarez, of Maximilian, and now of Juarez again, he had managed to keep his head above water.

King contacted his attorney Stephen Powers to try to make peace with his old enemy. Mifflin Kenedy joined them in trying to strike a deal that would allow their ranches to operate without the continued rustling. A pardon for Cortinas passed the Texas Senate but was tabled indefinitely in the House.

Although there is no proof that the brigadier of the Bravo actually stole cattle or ordered anyone else to steal it, he received it and handled it. He stocked four Tamaulipas ranches including his own famous Canelo with cattle and horses stolen from Texas. He filled contracts for Cuba with rustled beeves. In short, he got very rich.

Even the death of Juarez in 1872 did not end his regime. Even though everyone knew Cortinas was a thief, he was bringing prosperity to Tamaulipas. The Mexicans were willing to overlook his crimes against "the devil Texans." Mexico City left him in power.

Likewise, collusion probably existed between Matamoros and Austin because the state police of E. J. Davis seldom ventured into the Nueces Strip.

Probably more than half the cattle Cortinas received were branded with the Running W. As his greed grew insatiable, King and Kenedy as well as other ranchers in the Nueces Strip continued to lose incredible numbers of livestock to vicious raiders.

On September 13, 1873, King acquired the first title to the *San Juan Carricitos*. He had just sold his cattle for a good price in Abilene. Six days later the cattle market crashed. Not only cattle, but the entire stock market took a tumble. Credit tightened. Prices plunged.

Smaller spreads gave up in disgust. Mifflin Kenedy managed to sell *Los Laureles* and move his family to Corpus Christi. With the Comanche raiding as viciously in West Texas as the Mexicans in South Texas, the ranching industry looked to be going the way of the cotton kingdom.

King never once considered selling anything.

W W W

Nothing lasts forever. Particularly in politics. In 1873 Texas managed to hold a fairly honest election for governor.

Confederate veteran Richard Coke won, but Davis applied to President Ulysses S. Grant to declare martial law.

Grant bore no love for the South. The year before he had ordered bayonets to overturn an election in Louisiana. He regretted what he had done only because his actions had cost him a great measure of his popularity. The whole country was tired of punishing the South. He had to think of the congressional elections ahead. He refused.

Still Davis remained in his office in the capitol, refusing to vacate the premises and declaring that Coke's election was fraudulent.

On January 15, 1874, he looked out his window to see Texas arms stacked against him. Old Rip Ford, tall and handsome at sixty, marched up the street at the head of a disciplined body of men, many from his old Cavalry of the West. They were singing "The Yellow Rose of Texas."

Knowing he had no chance to remain, Davis vacated his office Monday, January 19, 1874.

King began to plan for a huge trail drive. Better to sell the cattle at reduced prices than have them stolen by Cheno Cortinas' *bandidos*.

ꟽ ꟽ ꟽ

The next year saw the beginning of the end for the rustlers. One of Governor Coke's first acts was to reinstitute the Texas Rangers.

One of the infamous state police, Leander McNelly, as a young man, had really cared about protecting the state's citizens. As a newly appointed Ranger captain, he rode into the King Ranch in 1875. He announced he was looking for bandits mounted on Dick Heye saddles. They were much prized and very expensive. Every Texan wanted one and could recognize one instantly by the burnished silver *conchos* decorating the saddle skirts.

They'd been stolen from Sol Lichtenstein's general store in Corpus Christi. In hopes of getting the saddles back, Sol had outfitted all forty-two Rangers with Sharps carbines. King blinked at the sight of the buffalo guns, and his *Kineños* muttered and whistled in amazement.

The 50-caliber bore was big enough for a gopher to crawl into, and the flat-nosed bullet was as big as a man's thumb. They were single shots, so the Rangers didn't get but one chance. That was the way Captain McNelly wanted it. "Hit what you aim at with the Sharps," he instructed, "and you don't have to shoot it twice."

The horses his men rode, however, were the sorriest of the sorry. For two days they'd traveled at a snail's pace, covering only twelve miles over cleared level ground of the Tex-Mex Railroad. In the latest of his diversification efforts, King had been responsible for building a line connecting Corpus Christi with Laredo where the Mexican railroad deadheaded. When the Rangers had ridden past the trestle, they'd seen two corpses hanging from it.

Such "executions" were one small example of the depredations Cortinas was responsible for. Federal commissioners had already reported to Washington that "Old and young were subjected to every form of outrage and torture, dragged at the hooves of horses, burned and flayed alive, shot to death, or cut to pieces with knives."

As the Rangers rode into the King Ranch they saw the changes that twenty years had wrought. From the adobe *jacál* where Henrietta had spent her honeymoon, the ranch house had grown to a two-story structure with a tower seventy-five feet high. Two lookouts manned it at all times. The Rangers had been seen, and scouts had ridden out to take a look.

The Rangers were escorted to some outbuildings, and Captain King himself rode out to take charge.

George Durham, a teenaged Ranger from Georgia, recalls the sight of King. "He wasn't much to look at. He was a dead ringer for Captain McNelly at a short distance. Neither of them looked like a storybook captain of anything. But they were. Both of them."

Durham also noted that the Santa Gertrudis ranch house was more like an army arsenal inside. In one large room were eighty stands of Henry repeating rifles and maybe a hundred boxes of shells. If the alarm were given from the watchtower, enough men to fire every one of those rifles were always close enough to come running.

ሥ ሥ ሥ

Captain King looked at McNelly's horses and shook his head. "How in the world did you get this far on those nags?" he asked. "You must have had to walk some."

"They're all we had," Captain McNelly said, "and the main fact is—we're here."

They were invited to spend the night. They ate in the dining hall that young Durham referred to as the "grub shanty." Its four long tables would seat maybe a hundred. They filed by and filled their mess kits with good beef stew and got a cup of coffee. Mrs. King and a young girl refilled the coffee whenever they wanted.

George Durham fell in love in that minute with the young girl who was Henrietta's niece—Caroline Chamberlain. He said he would have drunk cup after cup of coyote poison if she had refilled it for him. He resolved then and there to marry her if she'd have him. He swore to himself that he'd work hard and be a foreman.

Caroline was down at the corrals the next morning to see Captain King speak to one of his *vaqueros*, who dropped a rope on a good, rangy sorrel gelding and brought him up.

He also examined George's saddle and gave him a new one and a rifle scabbard.

The captain had noticed Caroline's interest in George and his moony eyes on her. He made George "one happy young 'un."

When George asked Captain King how much the horse and saddle were worth, Captain King said, "Don't let that bother you, son. Wherever Captain McNelly sends you, that horse will take you. He's a good, solid animal. Plenty of stay, and enough speed."

Captain King also put Captain McNelly on a horse named Segal, which McNelly judged to be worth $500.

When McNelly protested that the state of Texas would never pay what that horse was worth, Captain King said the same thing as Sol Lichtenstein in Corpus Christi. "I'd rather give him to you than have those bandits come and take him. Most of those rascals are mounted on my stock, and I at least want to do as good by you, Captain."

King's generosity was legendary by that time, particularly when he could see the advantage to himself. The Rangers had to be well mounted and well armed if they were to be able to make inroads against the murderous *bandidos* that had plagued Texas for so many years. In the same way he had kept the supplies moving for the Confederacy, King sent the Rangers into battle to win.

The Last Battles

Captain Leander McNelly was only thirty-one years old and a consumptive. He had a soft voice, an even temper, and cold steel disdain for personal danger. He was a brilliant leader who commanded the respect of the men he enlisted to ride with him. To a man they were young and idealistic. Their first sergeant was John Armstrong. The youngest, George Durham, was a nineteen-year-old Georgia farm boy.

Outfitted by Sol Lichtenstein and Richard King, the force of forty-two was formidable. As they rode down the trail from the Santa Gertrudis, they knew they were riding into a burst of rustling activity. Cortinas had already made a fortune delivering livestock to the Spanish garrison in Cuba. A ship for another such delivery was waiting at Boca del Rio.

In addition to the rustling, Cortinas' men had engaged in a reign of terror throughout the Nueces Strip. Five small ranches had been burned near La Parra on the upper Laguna Madre. The inhabitants had been killed and their cattle run off.

Fourteen miles north of Brownsville, on the Palo Alto prairie where so much blood had already been spilled,

McNelly came upon a dozen rustlers driving three hundred stolen cattle toward the river.

He struck like Rip Ford before him. The blazing fight lasted only a few minutes. One Ranger was killed, but not a single rustler got away alive. Next day, McNelly dumped their dead bodies in the market square in Brownsville.

They were identified as some of Cortinas' most notorious *bravos*. Their bodies flung in the dust sent a message to the rest of their kind. The Texas Rangers were back.

For five months thereafter, the border saw no major encounters while both sides maneuvered for positions. Cortinas enlisted spies among the *rancheros*. McNelly paid Mexicans for information. In November the Ranger captain learned that Las Cuevas outside Camargo was the gathering point for eighteen thousand head of Texas cattle to be delivered to Monterrey in three months.

McNelly got a promise from Major A. J. Alexander at Fort Ringgold that Alexander's men would follow McNelly wherever he would lead. If Santos Benavides had still been stationed there, no promise would have been necessary.

Expecting that Alexander's men would cross the river when they heard the first shots, McNelly confidentally led his men across the Rio Grande. At first dawn, they pulled the bars on the corral gates. The Rangers charged in yelling like banshees. Four Mexicans chopping wood were killed instantly.

To McNelly's horror he discovered he'd made a mistake. His men had not attacked Las Cuevas, but the outlying *rancho* of Cachattus. By the time they got to Las Cuevas, two hundred mounted Mexican soldiers had dashed into the stronghold.

McNelly retreated to the riverbank. The soldiers followed. A skirmish occurred. Alexander sent Captain Randlett of D Company, Eighth Cavalry across the river with forty troopers. With McNelly's troop they now numbered about seventy. Barely half were mounted.

As luck would have it, McNelly's fire had left a dead man in the open field. He was the *jefe* of Las Cuevas himself, General Juan Flores. Moreover, the Mexicans had seen that the U.S. Cavalry would cross the river. Suddenly, cattle stealing did not seem nearly so easy nor so attractive as it once had been.

McNelly tried in vain to get the thousands of cattle back. In the end only seventy-five were returned. Those came after McNelly stuck his cocked pistol in the face of the *caporál* and said through the interpreter, "tell the son-of-a-bitch that if he doesn't deliver the cattle across the river in less than five minutes, I'll kill every one of them."

Half wore the Running W on their sides. McNelly put George Durham and four other Rangers in charge of returning those cattle to Captain King.

When George arrived with the cattle, the ladies invited the boys to dinner. George reported that he was ashamed because he hadn't been barbered in months, his clothes were in rags, and he was filthy. Everything was provided so that he and his fellows could eat their supper in comfort. And what a supper it was—ham, eggs, butter, cakes, pies, fresh buttermilk and coffee, and two cakes baked by Ella and Nettie. A card read:

COMPLIMENTS OF THE TWO MISS KINGS
TO
THE McNELLY RANGERS

The willingness of the McNelly Rangers to invade Mexico and the support of the U.S. Cavalry spelled the end for Cheno Cortinas. Like Richard King and Rip Ford, the men he'd fought so long, he was getting old.

To his embarrassment Porfirio Diáz passed over him and chose a new commander who hated Cortinas. Cheno was arrested summarily but pardoned and allowed to retire to Canelo, the ranch he had acquired with his rustling money. He was allowed to grow old in peace and quiet, no doubt regaling his *niños* with stories of his exciting adventures and recalling the glorious enemies he had fought against.

In 1877 when McNelly died of consumption, Richard King had a decent monument of granite erected over his grave.

ꟿ ꟿ ꟿ

What King did for McNelly was much less than what he did for his friend Old Rip Ford. The old commander had outfitted much of the Cavalry of the West out of his own pocket, and because much of his soldiering had been done without benefit of Confederate or United States commissions, he had no pension. E. J. Davis's Reconstruction had treated him badly. Finally, he was over sixty with a family to support.

Beginning in 1865, an agent had come to Ford's landlord and said no rent was to be collected for Ford's home ever again. Days later a banker came with the news that at the beginning of every month $250 would be paid into Ford's account.

Ford never knew who paid it, but his daughter found out after his death. The benevolence had come from Richard King.

ꟿ ꟿ ꟿ

They were growing old together, friends and enemies, who had carved great places for themselves out of the land they rode over and in the history of that land. They accepted their aging as the natural progress of their lives.

King could see a smooth road ahead. To his credit, he never forgot his friends who didn't.

After a quarter of a century, he had wealth and prosperity beyond his wildest dreams. He owned a ranch of hundreds of thousands of acres, a ranch made up of ranchos whose names are testamentary to the terrible heritage of *El Desierto de los Muertos*—the land nobody wanted. *Rincón de Santa Gertrudis, De la Garza Santa Gertrudis, Los Sauces, Rincón del Grullo, La Boveda, El Pasadizo, Miguel Gutierrez Santa Gertrudis, Paso Ancho de Abajo, San Leandro, Agua Dulce, San Antonio de Agua Dulce, Los Presenos*, and *San Juan Carricitos*. He had created four mammoth ranches made out of dozens and dozens of acquisitions small and large. Every one was bought and paid for.

And nothing had been sold.

~ ~ ~

In 1878 King's first "Pet," Nettie, married Major E. B. Atwood of the U.S. Army. She was twenty-two years old and able to make her own decisions. Nevertheless, King must have been shocked. Only a few short years before, he'd dandled her on his knee.

Now she was marrying—a Yankee. Had the Civil War really been over so short a time? With Henrietta beside him, he did the gracious thing. Besides turning Parlor 17 in the Lindell Hotel into a "garden of flowers," he and Henrietta gave her $10,000 worth of gifts, "the handsomest [presents] ever given to a St. Louis bride."

As the grandchildren began to arrive and Henrietta spent more time in St. Louis, he wrote to her, "See that none of Papa's pets wants for anything that money will buy."

The year 1881 saw the first wedding at the ranch. Ella married a St. Louis and San Antonio merchant Louis M. Welton. Richard King was hurt and disappointed when he learned that they too planned to live in St. Louis. He had never considered that they wouldn't all live together at the ranch.

Did he have that thought in his mind in 1882 when he brought in a new lawyer he had hired in Corpus Christi? For a retainer of five thousand dollars a year, he brought home Robert Justus Kleberg. King's youngest daughter, nineteen-year-old Alice, was home from school at the time. When she saw the handsome young lawyer, she immediately set her cap for him.

King must have been pleased to see them together. At least *she* wouldn't move farther away than Corpus Christi.

In 1882 King's old lawyer Stephen Powers died after a long and successful career as a representative for King in all his legal dealings, as a state legislator, and as a judge. Although King's old business dealings were still handled by Powers's young partner James B. Wells, Robert Kleberg took over all new business.

Everyone expects to grow old and to see old friends die until their turn comes. But the unnaturalness of the death of children rocked both Richard and Henrietta to their very foundations.

In 1882 Henrietta's half brother Bland, the one among the Chamberlain boys who had planned to make a life for himself on the ranch, died suddenly of a fever at age thirty-three. The unfairness of his loss seemed to sap King's strength.

The Captain was fifty-eight years old, and now his body seemed to fail him. Although he blamed it on age, he was in pain. His stomach hurt, and he resorted more and more to Rose Bud whiskey as a palliative.

For the first time he looked at obstacles that seemed too great for him to overcome. His pastures were overstocked. A drought was burning up the Wild Horse Desert. The lack of vigor in his own body left him with the feeling that it was all too much.

Then in February 1883, he and Henrietta received the news that their younger son Robert E. Lee was ill of pneumonia in St. Louis. The family started north immediately. By the time they reached him, his condition was grave. He died in March 1883 and was buried in a St. Louis cemetery far from the Santa Gertrudis that he had planned to operate for his father.

Henrietta was so grief stricken that she became seriously ill and had to stay in St. Louis with Ella and Nettie for several months. Alice returned with her father to attend to affairs on the ranch.

The loss was insupportable for Richard King. For the first time, he considered selling the ranch. In April he wrote to his wife: "I am tired of the business."

He actually went so far as to list the ranch with a realtor. A syndicate announced an interest, but the price for ranch and stock was $6,500,000. Perhaps he actually set it so high so no one would buy it. The syndicate was frightened away. No one else could come close to affording the vastness of Wild Horse Desert.

By June he was back to worrying about his stock and about Mrs. King. He missed her terribly. Then in July the rains fell and he began to be hopeful again.

His son Richard married Pearl Ashbrook, and Richard King I and Henrietta gave him a Deed of Gift out "of Love and Affection"—forty thousand acres comprising the *Rancho Puerta de Agua Dulce*. On the "Sweet Water" Captain King built them an elegant new house and more or less supported Richard's poor business dealings.

In 1884 Alice became engaged to Robert Justus Kleberg, whose practice consisted mainly of the King Ranch. The Captain must have smiled behind his hand and chuckled to himself. At least one of his "Pets" would remain at the Santa Gertrudis and rear his grandchildren there.

But by the year's end, the Captain was sick and infinitely tired. He was sixty years old. His coats hung loose from his shoulders. His black beard and hair were peppered with gray. Pain now gnawed at him continuously. Still, he drove himself relentlessly, letting his will command even when his body could no longer function.

He was never without whiskey. Yet he wouldn't go to a doctor. He knew what a doctor would say.

One beam of happiness came at Christmastime. His grandson Richard King III was born on December 17.

In January King returned from a business trip in Corpus Christi and staggered into the Santa Gertrudis ranch house. He could drive his body no longer. A month later Henrietta and Alice were able to persuade him to go to a doctor in San Antonio.

February 25 he dictated a letter to Reuben Holbein to contact Jim Wells in Brownsville with regard to a piece of land attached to the *San Juan Carricitos*. "Tell him to keep on buying. And tell him, tell him not to let a foot of the dear old Santa Gertrudis get away from us—"

Nothing was left to say. Spring was a hard time to leave the ranch he loved, but he had no choice. With his wife and daughter supporting him, he came out of the house and down the steps. He shook a few hands—never so many as he would have wished. He was helped inside. The coach pulled away.

He never came back.

The time had come for King to fight his last battle. It was fitting that he return to a place where heroes had left their blood.

They took him to a suite on the second floor of the Menger Hotel, where his room looked out on the Alamo. The doctor came to him and diagnosed what King had already known—stomach cancer. No operation was possible.

On one occasion he heard Henrietta weeping. She needed him, she said. She didn't want him to leave her.

He got up and put on his pants. "I won't leave you, Pet. Not if you still need me."

But he was in too much pain. In the end she had to let him go.

On April 14, 1885, as dusk fell on the Plaza across from the Alamo, King breathed his last.

No one could have had a better life.

The Myth

The Hunters

As she pushed the dishtowel into a glass, it slipped from her nervous fingers and shattered on the kitchen floor. Their son set up a howl of indignation, but she didn't dare dash toward the bedroom. Her feet were bare.

Carefully, she stepped back. The linoleum was gritty under foot, but she managed the first step without any damage. On the second she was unlucky. A curved shard sliced into her left heel. She had to bend over to pull it out. When she did, she cut her index finger.

She knew exactly what her husband meant when he cursed.

She dropped into a chair and used the dishtowel to blot her heel while she sucked her finger. The baby kept on crying—now hiccuping between sobs. She called to him trying to soothe him with meaningless words while she did what she should have done to begin with. With the dishtowel, she mopped a clear path through the splinters.

Leaving little drops of blood with every step, she padded into the bedroom. The baby stopped crying immediately when she picked him up and placed him on her shoulder. He tucked his sweet face into her neck and rested his baby arm under her chin.

A rifle barked far off in the distance. She started and clutched him tight. The shacks of the Humble Oil field houses at Willamar had paper thin walls. Then she remembered. She'd heard another shot. That was the sound that had made her drop the glass.

She clutched the baby tighter. The stinging had all but stopped in her foot. Her finger had stopped bleeding. That meant that the wounds were closing. She wouldn't have to get out the gauze and adhesive tape.

She wished her husband wouldn't hunt. He and his brother were like little boys going out with toy guns. They didn't even particularly like venison. They just liked to go out at three in the morning, sit in a thicket, and wait for some poor unsuspecting animal to come by. Or creep through the underbrush in the first rays of dawn hoping to scare up some wild creature.

That in itself wasn't dangerous. But where they hunted was danger itself. Everyone knew that. Her neighbor from next door, visiting in the kitchen, had told how the King Ranch didn't allow hunters on their land. Not at all. Nary a one.

The neighbor's eyes got big, but she nodded her head as if she'd done her duty. For nearly a hundred years, King and his heirs the Klebergs had had to fight rustlers. Sometimes their own people had been killed by them. Sometimes hunters would ride through the fences and shoot the big red Santa Gertrudis cattle and claim they'd killed them by mistake.

So the ranchers didn't tolerate them anymore. Not anyone, anytime, anywhere.

The woman had seen the fence riders with rifles in their saddle boots and pistols on their hips. The hot-eyed, dark-skinned men, stone-faced, serious, sat their horses as if the two were one. She'd shuddered a little at the sight of the pistols even though she was used to the rifles and shotguns her husband owned.

She'd begged and pleaded, but he'd smiled a little and kissed and patted her. They'd never catch him and his brother. They'd be in and out before the fence riders could figure out where the shots came from.

Then real trouble had come calling. The Willacy County sheriff and his deputy had come by. She hadn't heard what they'd said. They'd just asked him to get in the car and take a ride.

What they said, he never told. But his face was red as fire and the veins stood out over the clenched muscles in his forearms.

For weeks he hadn't gone hunting. Until tonight.

She'd heard the shots. Two now.

She put the baby back in his crib and went out on the front porch. A nighthawk dipped across the moon. In the mesquite trees bats fluttered about, squeaking as they caught their dinners. She sat down on the porch stoop next to the little pots of red geraniums. Absently, she broke off some of the withered clusters of blossoms so more would bloom.

Another shot. Her hand crushed the withered flowers. She couldn't be sure she hadn't destroyed live blossoms. Her hand might have slipped.

Suddenly, the night was shattered by a fusillade. She sprang to her feet. One-two—three, then four and five. She wrapped her arms around the four-by-four that supported the little porch and hung on for dear life.

Deer didn't shoot back, nor wild turkey, nor javelina.

The guns of the fence riders—she could see them clearly in her mind's eye. She pushed her fist against her teeth.

All she could do was pray, but she feared prayer was already too late.

He didn't come back. Days passed, nearly a week. He and his brother disappeared utterly.

With her baby in her arms, she went to the sheriff, who shrugged his big shoulders. What did she really know?

All she'd heard was shots.

Shots could mean anything. Could she say where they'd come from?

She couldn't say for sure.

No Trespassing signs were up on all the fences, but if it'd make her feel better, he promised to ride out and take a look around. She wanted to scream at him that murder had been done, but without a body, nobody could say for sure.

He looked at her with her plain Sears, Roebuck dress, her bare feet in her old sandals, her straight brown hair, caught back at the side with a barrette. His gaze dropped to the baby boy cradled in her arms.

"Maybe he just wasn't man enough to take responsibility."

Her face went white. She stumbled to her feet and hurried out the door. She'd said all she could, done all she could. And not only had she been insulted, but her husband's memory had been insulted as well.

She took the baby boy to bed beside her because she was so lonely. Sleepless one night, she thought she heard the shots again. She sat bolt upright in bed. Her son lay sleeping quietly beside her.

After reassuring herself that he was all right, she rose. When her heel struck the floor, it stung. As if she'd just that instant pulled the shard of glass from it, it stung. By the time she reached the front porch, her finger was stinging too. The moon was dark that night, a pale sliver holding a single star in its cradle.

A chill trickled down her spine. A devil moon. Horns. She wanted to run back inside and pull the covers up over her head. Instead, she waited.

If she'd really heard them, she'd hear more. She couldn't say how she knew, but she waited, shivering in the warm humid air.

There they were! She counted five.

Why was this happening?

Because the dead called for vengeance. She knew he was dead. She pictured him, a pale ghost rising from the shallow grave where the fence riders had thrown him.

She covered her eyes with her hands. Tears trickled through her fingers. She couldn't be sure, but she thought her finger was bleeding. *Oh, no. Oh, no. I can't. I really can't.*

She couldn't help him. She couldn't go to the sheriff. He'd laugh at her this time.

She couldn't go.

The wind stirred. The trees rattled. The bats squeaked louder than ever, then fell silent. Everywhere was silence.

She tried to find the courage to drop her hands. She couldn't. She didn't want to see what she feared. She'd never feared him in life, but she feared him in death.

So she remained, bent over her knees on the front stoop with her hands covering her eyes.

Gradually, the night sounds returned. She knew he was gone. Quietly, she lowered her hands, rose, and went back to bed.

The next night the same thing happened, but still she couldn't look.

And the next. And the next.

She couldn't look, but she couldn't bear this anymore. She was going mad. With her baby in her arms, she went to the sheriff. In a flat voice that didn't sound like her own, she told what had happened. When she finished, she asked the lawman to drive out and see what he could find.

He didn't answer.

She raised her eyes.

He couldn't meet them. His mouth twitched as if he were chewing on something bitter. He stared out the window. His beefy hands clutched the chair arms.

And then she knew. She couldn't do a thing about it, but she knew. She rose and crossed to the door. Her mother had made a place for them in her old bedroom. She was taking the baby and going home

"I'll leave him to you," she said in the same flat voice. "And you to him."

Part V

"As I Myself Might Do"

The Truth

Aftermath

If ever the Fates spun a golden thread, it was for the life of Richard King. No heroes in epic literature achieved more. Indeed they achieved less, for in him was a combination of ruler and hero, shaper of the empire and ruthless instrument of the gods. By will, by strength, by intelligence, in the space of thirty years, he carved a kingdom that rivaled the principalities of Europe.

All America took note of his death. Thousands of miles away, the New York newspapers reported the death of the "Texas Millionaire Richard King." As much as any of the military heroes of the Mexican and Civil Wars, they marked his passing as the passing of an era.

And so it was.

Henrietta Chamberlain King was devastated and sorely afraid. All her life a strong man had shared her confidences, smoothed her way, allowed her to live a life of ease. She presided over a gracious home with elegant furnishings, fine clothes, adoring servants, happy visits to her children and grandchildren.

From the choir of Hiram Chamberlain's Presbyterian church, she had gone to her husband's Santa Gertrudis

Ranch and by his side into the world of the rich and powerful. She had never been alone.

Even more frightening was the commandment from her husband as set down in his will. He had bequeathed her everything "to be used by her and disposed of precisely the same as I myself might do were I living."

Not to a prince or princesses did he leave this dictum, but to his queen. To act as "I myself might do."

She was a woman who took command. Like the grand dame she had become, she assumed the responsibilities. She was fifty-three years old and in excellent health. She had survived the greatest tragedies that could befall a woman in any times: death of father, of brother, of son, of husband.

Duty was the way she had lived her life to that point. In duty she would continue to do so. She copied out a credo and pasted the words on a page in the scrapbook she kept as most women did in those days.

What I Live For

I live for those who love me
For all human ties that bind me
For the good that I may do.

But, oh, she missed her Captain.

The worth of the King Ranch was incalculable so far as the land, the water, and the mineral rights were concerned. Incalculable in so far as the wealth of the future contained therein.

In terms of money as bankers and tax collectors might assess, the real estate was worth somewhat more than half a million dollars. The livestock was worth somewhat less. The widow was left an estate with the official appraised value of $1,061,484.

She was also left with nearly half a million dollars' worth of debts. The list began with Francisco Yturria and went on and on. Some were large, some were small. Not that King had been profligate. He owed nothing that a man in the midst of business might not have on his books. He was in the business of acquiring land, buying and selling stock, diversifying his operations. Even though he knew he was sick, he did not expect to die. He left all this business to his widow.

At the instruction of Robert Kleberg, Alice King's fiancé, Jim Wells of Brownsville, the junior partner of the late Stephen Powers, devised a list of men to whom King owed money. He sent letters to each one advising them that Mrs. King was assuming the debts of her husband. They were to rest assured that the debts would be paid.

As executrix of her husband's estate, Henrietta spent nearly ten years paying everyone, but she did so even when old friends excused her. She did so even though at one point she had to sell part of the land. As she did, she trembled. Her husband's last words had been to buy more. To pay the debts was part and parcel of the kind of life she was determined to live. She was fortunate in the kind of son-in-law King had picked for her.

ʍ ʍ ʍ

Robert Justus Kleberg II was born on a family farm near Meyersville, Texas, on December 5, 1853. His grandparents and his mother had fled from Santa Anna in the "Runaway Scrape," across Texas. His father, Robert Justus Kleberg I, had joined up as a private in Sam Houston's army. At San Jacinto he had distinguished himself by his bravery. He was one of three men selected by Sam Houston to guard the Mexican dictator, General Antonio Lopez de Santa Anna.

In 1885 Robert Kleberg II became ranch manager of the Santa Gertrudis. In June 1886 he married King's daughter Alice Gertrudis in a private ceremony at six in the morning.

Captain Mifflin Kenedy gave the bride away in place of her father. He could barely stifle the tears as he remembered his dearest old friend. He couldn't forget that he was the elder of the two.

The happy couple left by stage for the railhead in Corpus Christi. As a mark of how much Alice loved her mother and how much Robert Kleberg admired and respected Henrietta, they took her with them on their summer honeymoon.

Facing life without her Captain, Henrietta donned mourning black. Every one of the *Kineños* approved the tribute she paid him. Through all the long, lonely space of almost forty years of widowhood, she never set aside her black garments.

When the three returned at the end of the summer they were all renewed. They had agreed that Robert Kleberg would assume management of the Santa Gertrudis. He had convinced the two women in his life that he was capable of doing so, but he had much harder judges to convince—the *Kineños*.

Nearly three hundred of them were men who rode almost as soon as they could walk—something he did not. They worked the cow camps and the corrals. They answered to the foremen and the *caporales*. They would not easily give their loyalty to a German lawyer with a big moustache, especially one who spoke no Spanish.

Kleberg was ready for them. A sharp, perceptive man, he understood the way things worked on the Santa Gertrudis. The ranch was a patriarchy, and he had been handed the role of *El Patrón*. He could never be *El Señor Capitan*, but he had to take the responsibility that his *gente*, his people, expected of him.

They watched him, their black eyes fierce with the unfailing stare of hawks. They were the men and the sons of the men who had made the *entrada* with Captain King. He was the son-in-law of *La Patrona*.

Robert was fair, he was smart, and he was determined to carry on after the great man. The Santa Gertrudis would not sink into obscurity and be sold off as unprofitable. It would grow and prosper with the changing times. He would not be hasty. He would study and learn, then when he gave orders he would expect to be obeyed.

He knew he had been accepted in his own right when he heard they had named him. He was *El Abogado*, The Lawyer.

The first change Kleberg made was to stop the cattle drives to Kansas. After the Civil War railroad lines pushed into Texas. He utilized them. Unfortunately, many railroad lines snaked across the rest of the western states and territories of the United States. Their cattle were also available to the stockyards of the big cities. Too many cattle caused the prices to be lower. In fact, the bottom dropped out of the market.

The years 1886 and 1887 were terrible years for Henrietta and Robert. They made little progress paying off King's debts. Besides the low market prices, the semidesert experienced another drought.

The cattle could not be sold because the market had dried up. The cattle could not drink because the land dried up. The ranch became a true desert of the dead.

The combination of these two disasters caused Kleberg to issue his first major order—a cleaning out of the Santa Gertrudis breeding pasture enclosed in the monstrous board fence, the first one Captain King had built.

Since the pasture had not been worked for several seasons, the great herd had bred unmolested and unbranded. The cattle in it were wild and dangerous. Francisco Alvarado's son Ramon took five weeks to make the roundup. Even with such a formidable man at the head of the *vaqueros*, bunches of the wildest cattle ran like deer through the *brasada*. Horses were killed or hurt every day in the process of roping and castrating the wild bulls. One *vaquero* was gored.

While the *Kineños* risked their lives, Kleberg began a program that would eventually see that they never had to do so again. The longhorns had outlived their usefulness. Since they no longer were to be driven to market, a heavier, more domesticated breed could be introduced. More meat on the hoof meant more money at the packing plant.

He bought shorthorn bulls from breeding farms in Texas, Kansas, Mississippi, Kentucky, Illinois, and even Canada to begin a new era of cattle raising on the King Ranch.

To import these cattle was expensive. The only way Kleberg could do this was with the approval of his mother-in-law. He never had to worry. He was backed every step of the way by Henrietta King. Her Captain had worked all his life to improve the ranch. She was pleased that her son-in-law did the same.

Indeed, she loved the pretty shorthorns. She considered them very civilized alongside the wild longhorns. Also she and her daughter found they were particularly partial to red cattle.

Unfortunately, the shorthorns did not do well. Henrietta, as well as everyone else on the ranch, could only watch unhappily as most of them sickened and died within the first year.

When the beautiful shorthorns arrived they had fine, glossy coats. Soon afterwards, they would be covered with cattle ticks. So many insects sucking blood from an animal was enough to make it sick, but worse than that was the Texas Fever.

The disease had caused the old longhorn herds to be blocked out of Kansas during the last years of the cattle drives. "Winchester quarantines" were the order of the day along the Kansas border. Kansas farmers and ranchers turned back the longhorns and the drovers with rifles when they saw that everywhere the Texas cattle walked, Kansas herds caught the fever and died.

Kleberg, a lawyer and the son of a judge, was equally interested in science. He reasoned that the ticks were causing the fatal disease. Clever and well connected as King had been, Robert sought a way to get his theories tested free. He interested U.S. Secretary of Agriculture J. M. Rusk in using the cattle of the King Ranch as the laboratory specimens for a scientific study.

In 1889 Dr. Cooper Curtice of the Bureau of Animal Industry arrived at the ranch. He stayed for three years studying the cattle tick. His work soon pointed to a microscopic parasite that attacked the red corpuscles of cattle. It lived in the cattle tick, which transmitted Texas Fever to the new shorthorn cattle. Unlike the longhorn, they hadn't had generations of natural selection to build immunity.

When his first observations and experiments brought hopeful results, Henrietta King seized an opportunity. Range land prices had fallen as ranchers without King Ranch resources and credit wanted out of the business. For fifty and seventy-five cents an acre, she was able to buy back almost all the land she had been forced to sell.

How relieved and exultant she must have felt. She had not lost any of her husband's land.

In 1891 Kleberg himself invented and put into use at the Santa Gertrudis the world's first cattle dipping vat, a long chute-like tank fitted with an approach-way. A cowpuncher then forced the animal onto a swinging door that dropped open and dipped the cow completely in an arsenical solution that would kill the ticks but not injure cattle. Good results were obtained immediately from this process.

Kleberg's second order was to rid the ranch of the huge herd of worthless wild mustangs from which the Wild Horse Desert took its name. In times of drought every blade of grass was valuable, and these horses ate more than their share besides serving no useful purpose. Eventually, four thousand were run through a funnel-shaped entrance to a brush corral at Tulosa Lake. It was probably the largest band of wild horses ever caught anywhere at any one time.

Teams of *vaqueros* drove them around and around, without rest. After ten days of continual driving, they were so weakened that they were manageable. One whole trainload of them was shipped to Mississippi and Tennessee, where Kleberg traded them for a few head of well-bred, gentle horses.

Can you find the longhorns? Three big steers graze among the mesquite trees behind the King Ranch wire fence. Such protective coloration made the cattle difficult to spot and capture. (Author photo)

The years 1891 and 1892 further drove ranchers out of business as a particularly hellish drought wracked South Texas. It was called “the great die-up” and is remembered as the most severe drought the Wild Horse Desert ever experienced. Hundreds of head of both longhorns and shorthorns died beside the dried-up waterholes. One *vaquero* recalled that he skinned seven hundred head of dead cattle. Although cattle prices were also low throughout those years, the hides were still worth something for leather.

With the tick problem at least partially solved and the wild horses eliminated, Kleberg ordered new cattle. He trusted these cattle to his new ranch foreman, Samuel G. Ragland. The young man brought the first herd of twelve hundred shorthorns from Grayson County just south of the Red River to Kingsville, six hundred miles, without a single animal lost.

In 1892 the King Ranch began to gain nationwide prominence. The ranch house on the rise above the Santa Gertrudis had been enlarged and refurbished for Robert and Alice Kleberg. One story had become two with pillars and lattice railing on the outside galleries that ran along both the first and second floors. The home was furnished with the beautiful antiques the Captain had bought for Henrietta, as well as fine furniture she had acquired on her trips to visit Alice’s sisters in St. Louis.

The Presbyterian minister’s daughter had come a long way from the *jacál* where she had spent her honeymoon. Her home was written about in *Harper’s Weekly* by Richard Harding Davis. From his article came the famous Texas tall tale that once an Easterner enters the front gate of a Texas ranch, he will still have miles to travel. In the case of the King Ranch, the distance to the front gate was indeed ten miles.

The article also described in detail Kleberg's business practices that enabled him to run a seven-hundred-thousand-acre property with one hundred thousand head of cattle. Another Texas saying was born: Everything is bigger in Texas.

In 1893 the result of the King Ranch study was published in the full report by the Bureau of Animal Industry pathologist, Dr. Theobald Smith. The cattle tick and the fever it spread were now thoroughly understood. The war of eradication could now be waged nationwide.

This major breakthrough in cattle raising occurred at the same time as a drop in the price of range land. Again Henrietta bought land for even lower prices per acre. Now the ranch totaled more acres than it had when King died. Moreover, not only did she buy more land, she made a profit as well.

In some circles she was criticized for her success. The Presbyterian minister's daughter was not behaving as a meek, debt-ridden widow. Instead, she was making profitable deals as her husband had before her. From that time on, she was regarded as a force to be reckoned with rather than an object of sympathy and pity.

For the first time since her Captain's death, she felt as if she was his true successor. In her secret Presbyterian heart, she experienced the sin of pride. She had added to her husband's ranch *as he himself would have done*. Her quiet pleasure at her success can only be imagined.

One whose praise meant everything to her was Captain Mifflin Kenedy. He had been responsible for bringing her husband to Texas. He had introduced the two of them and brought King to church. He had been a best friend and partner. Henrietta was heartbroken when Kenedy died of a heart attack on March 14, 1895, almost ten years to the day after King's death.

As before, Henrietta felt the passing of the years. Even though she was only sixty-three, younger than both of the captains, she perhaps felt her era was ending. Rather than take the chance that her Captain's ranch would be thrown into turmoil by her unexpected death, she gave her son-in-law her power of attorney for the handling of all legal and financial matters connected with the King Ranch. It was in effect for the remainder of her life.

Perhaps she really was tired. Maybe she looked back on her life since coming to the Rio Grande with her father at age seventeen as enough work for any person, man or woman. Perhaps she was satisfied that she had achieved what her Captain had asked of her.

More than likely she was content to take up the life she had always known. She made long trips to visit the families of her other children. She built herself a house in Corpus Christi where she could watch Alice's five children go to school and enjoy their progress. She entertained in a royal style both there and on the ranch.

In 1895, ten years after King's death, the debts were paid and the land was cleared of its overstocking. In short, everything and everyone seemed poised to move smoothly into a new and prosperous century.

Winning and Losing

The *Kineños* brought one thing from Cruillas that the entire ranch, indeed all of South Texas, regrets to this very day. All the battles fought against the Karankawa and Cheno Cortinas, against the Yankees and the drought have been victories. The enemy that has won and kept on winning is the mesquite.

The sons and grandsons of Richard King must keep fighting it to this very day. The *brasada* that it in large part created had become their enemy.

The mesquite is a thorny gnarled tree. Its branches spread out rather then grow up. Its rough limbs twist and dip to the ground where it continues to spread. Yet the long yellow bean pods it drops die on the harsh soil rather than germinate.

But if the mesquite beans are eaten by cattle or horses, such as the ones that King and his people brought from Mexico on his e*ntrada*, the animals pass the indigestible seeds through their digestive systems. The heat cracks the hulls. Eventually they fall to the ground again, this time mixed in a hospitable manure. Germination is rapid and inevitable.

So the mesquite tree crossed the Rio Grande and spread all across the Wild Horse Desert. Where it grew and spread its limbs along the ground, other thorny plants—cactus, huisache, ebony—sprouted under its protection. The grass was choked out. Less and less grazing was available for cattle.

Because of man's watchfulness, grass fires that once consumed acres of such thickets no longer scorched the land. Man further allowed intensive cattle grazing, which left pastures barren and vulnerable to encroachment. In short, at the dawn of the twentieth century the King Ranch was a limitless sea of grass no longer. Now it was engaged in a battle as fierce as any ever waged against *bandidos* or Yankees.

At first Kleberg hired transient workers to chop brush and grub roots with axes, picks, and grubbing hoes. They worked in gangs and were paid five dollars for every acre they cleared and fifty cents for each cord of wood they chopped. They were given weekly rations and could eat at the ranch commissary whenever they were not out in the gangs.

Fairly soon, Kleberg and his foreman, Sam Ragland, realized that manpower was too slow and the growth of the *brasada* too rapid. The answer must lie in technology. A huge steel harrow was constructed to root up the thickets. A discus followed it, slicing the uprooted trees and cactus into pieces. Still it was killing work—expensive and generally fairly ineffective. From the smallest root or the tiniest seed, a tree can sprout.

The battle continues to this very day. The *brasada* is a formidable enemy that will probably never be defeated.

Equally as terrible as the battle against the thickets was the battle against the recurring drought. Santa Gertrudis Creek offered the first fresh water Captain King encountered between the Rio Grande and the Nueces. One reason for overgrazing of the home pastures was the lack of standing or running water farther south. *El Señor Capitán* had often complained, "Where I have grass, I have no water. And where I have water, I have no grass."

Water wells were the answer, Kleberg was sure, but initial digging had struck saltwater or nothing. Reading and studying had found the cure for tick fever. Through them the ranch had engaged the battle with the *brasadas*. Reading and studying would find water.

In October 1898 Kleberg reported to Mrs. King that only twenty percent of their vast acreage was usable year round. He had read about a German at New Braunsfels who had dug successful artesian wells. He staked Theodore L. Herring to go to Nebraska to buy a heavy new rig with a new drilling bit. Herring returned with the Dempster No. 6 Combined Hydraulic Rotating and Cable Drilling Machine.

On a designated spot five miles north and west of the present town of Kingsville, Kleberg instructed Herring to keep on drilling until he struck water or came out on the other side. On the sixth of June 1899, a clear column of pure artesian drinking water burbled up from a depth of 532 feet. It poured out at the rate of seventy-five gallons a minute.

The dreaded aridity of the coming summer was effectively headed off by a half million gallons of pure water per day flowing into a huge stock tank. Over the years the ranch has continued to tap into the huge subterranean flow until today 320 wells dot the land. Today many are non-flowing, so windmills are also part of the ranch's landscape.

ꟿ ꟿ ꟿ

One of the most important additions to the Santa Gertrudis came in 1900. To usher in the new century a new man appeared—Caesar Kleberg, Robert's nephew. He had served for two years as his father's congressional secretary in Washington, D.C.

Ignorant of ranch life, he became the devoted pupil of Sam Ragland, who taught him about the cattle and particularly about the horses that he came to love. As if he were one of Richard King's own, he moved into the ranch house. To his five nephews and nieces, he became a beloved elder brother, a teacher, and eventually a role model.

Alice Gertrudis and Robert Justus Kleberg had five children—two boys and three girls. The first boy born in 1887 only two years after his grandfather's death was Richard Mifflin, named for Richard King and Mifflin Kenedy. In 1889 the first daughter was born and named Henrietta Rosa after her two grandmothers. In 1893 Alice Gertrudis was born and named for her mother. The second son, born in 1896, was named Robert Justus Kleberg Jr. The last child, a daughter born in 1898, was named Sarah Spohn after Mifflin Kenedy's daughter.

The *Kineños* watched all these children with pride and love, recognizing their position as heirs of the vital empire. They were the next generation for their own nation. They were no longer Mexicans, but they were not Americans either. And though it was named Santa Gertrudis, in their minds they were citizens of the King Ranch.

One of them was asked by a visitor if he liked working for Mr. Kleberg. The man replied that he didn't work for Mr. Kleberg. He worked for King Ranch. But it was Mr. Kleberg's ranch, the visitor argued. The *Kineño* shook his head. Mr. Kleberg, he declared, worked for King Ranch too.

The most eloquent and famous portrait of *Kineño* loyalty in the twentieth century comes fittingly enough from the true story of Ignacio Alvarado, a *caporál* and son of Francisco Alvarado, who had taken the bullet for King. Kleberg waited several days for Ignacio to come to the roundup. Without him, starting the work of the cow camp was unthinkable. Since the very first one, he had always been there setting the example for the men.

At last his son came riding into camp. Kleberg immediately wanted to know where his *caporál* was.

"My father said to tell you he was sorry he could not come," the boy replied. "He had to die."

ꟾ ꟾ ꟾ

No kingdom can function efficiently with its neighbors without transportation and communication. Nothing seemed more logical to Robert Kleberg. In January 1903 a corporation was formed for the purpose of building a railroad from Sinton in San Patricio County, south across Nueces, Hidalgo, and Cameron Counties 160 miles south to Brownsville. It was to be called the St. Louis, Brownsville, and Mexico Railroad. It was affectionately known as the "Brownie."

Without hesitation Henrietta King donated the right-of-way across her property, nearly one hundred of the required miles. Her Captain had planned to build a railroad. She was merely carrying on as he himself might have done. But greater things awaited her than he had ever dreamed.

Four months later Kleberg asked Henrietta to help him build a town three miles due east from the ranch house. Since it was in the heart of *El Rincón de Santa Gertrudis*, Henrietta again donated the land for the town. It would be called Kingsville. Its longest streets were to be named King Avenue and Santa Gertrudis Avenue. In order, north of King Avenue were Nettie, Ella, Richard, Alice, and Lee, the names of her five children in the order of their births. Her name came next.

Kenedy Avenue ran parallel to King. Kleberg was there. And Ragland. And Caesar. Armstrong and Wells.

With their names posted where people would walk among them, Henrietta could feel that their glory had not departed. Perhaps it would never depart. The construction began almost immediately.

She and her son-in-law owned the Kleberg Town & Improvement Company. She owned the Kingsville Lumber Company, the town's first business. She consulted with her city planner on how the streets should be laid out on the 853 acres she had donated. The sale of each lot for fifty dollars went to her. A strict clause was written into every bill of sale. Absolutely no liquor was to be for sale on the premises. She wanted no saloons in her town.

She donated the land and the funds required for construction of the first church, a Presbyterian, of course. In quick order, the Baptists, the Methodists, the Episcopalians, and the Catholics all came and were welcomed. She donated the land for all of them.

An already successful life was overflowing with blessings as she rode down to her new town site to meet the first train ever to make a scheduled run over the Wild Horse Desert. Her eyes filled with tears. The seventy-one-year-old lady stood up in the wagon and clasped her hands.

"Thank goodness, it is here!" she exclaimed.

She was issued Complimentary Pass No. 1. Complimentary Pass No. 2 was for Mrs. R. J. Kleberg & Children. The vice president and general manager of the railroad was Jeff N. Miller, whose name was given to another avenue in Kingsville. It was his pleasure to order a caboose hooked to an engine on Friday afternoons and sent into Corpus Christi.

After school the Kleberg children—Dick, who was seventeen, Henrietta, Alice, Bob, and six-year-old Sarah—found their own train waiting at the station to take them home for the weekend. At the depot in Kingsville, horses were waiting for them to gallop the three miles to the ranch. On Monday morning their journey was reversed. No young princes and princesses in Europe had more fun, and certainly none of them had as much happiness or freedom.

The run to Brownsville took an easy nine hours, in contrast to the jolting forty hours required to travel by stagecoach. North and southbound passenger trains ran six days a week. Henrietta objected to travel on the Sabbath. Freight trains ran three times a week.

A train much like this one made the first run across the Wild Horse Desert on the rails of the St. Louis, Brownsville, and Mexico Railroad. (From the Collections of the Texas/Dallas History and Archives Division, Dallas Public Library.)

Loading pens were built at intervals along the line, so Santa Gertrudis cattle could be loaded directly from the pastures into the cattle cars bound for packing houses in distant cities. Fifty miles down the line at Norias, Caesar Kleberg set up his headquarters. From there he bossed the lower end of the King Ranch for thirty years.

As King had diversified in every direction, so did Kleberg with Mrs. King backing him through every deal. Her Kingsville Publishing Company published a weekly newspaper. Her Kingsville Power and Light Company provided electricity. His Kingsville Ice and Milling Company brought ice to the town. She established the Gulf Coast Gin Company, which owned most of the gins in an area admirably suited to growing Sea Island Long Staple cotton.

The first public school opened in 1906 with thirteen pupils and one teacher. In 1909 Mrs. King donated grounds and seventy-five thousand dollars to build a twenty-two-room school.

Her fame spread beyond the borders of Texas. She became a *grande dame* in the eyes of the nation, and the ranch she headed became world famous. President William Howard Taft came to Corpus Christi to promise that the Corps of Engineers would soon begin work on improving the harbor to make it a deepwater port. After a brief speech, he retired to Henrietta's Broadway mansion for luncheon. Even though her hospitality was famous and she never turned anyone away at her commissary on the King Ranch, his consequence was elevated by his association with her.

ᨓ ᨓ ᨓ

In 1910 Brownsville awoke from its sleep. Suddenly, it was no longer only a port. It was a growing trading center at the end of a railroad. Its politicians turned greedy.

All of South Texas in those days was divided into Cameron, Hidalgo, and Nueces Counties. The King Ranch was divided between Cameron with Brownsville as its county seat and Nueces with Corpus Christi as its seat. City bond issues were funded by taxing land. The large populations of these two towns had little land, but they voted to tax the

Santa Gertrudis for the huge majority of county and municipal costs and improvements.

To save itself from being taxed into poverty, the Santa Gertrudis turned political. It lobbied Austin for nearly three years until four new counties were created. Jim Wells County was named for the family lawyer in Brownsville. Its county seat was named Alice for Alice Gertrudis Kleberg. Willacy County was named for their state senator John G. Willacy. Kenedy County was named for the King's longtime friend. The town of Kingsville became the county seat of Kleberg County. Taxes would thereafter go to the people who needed the services they paid for.

ᨓ ᨓ ᨓ

As well run and as protected as the King Ranch was, its pastoral idyll could not go on forever. At four A.M. on January 4, 1912, Henrietta King saw her glorious home go up in flames. Fire broke out within the old, dry wooden walls. The mansion went up like paper.

Dick Kleberg's dog awakened Caesar and Caesar's brother Al by barking and pulling at the bedcovers. In their nightshirts the men dashed out onto the second floor porch to awaken their cousins in the front of the house.

The Klebergs hurried down the stairs and out into the freezing air. Their houseguests, the Millers, had to climb out windows and slide down the outside porch to escape.

Intrepid as only a queen named King could be, Henrietta emerged from the burning house wearing a black dress and carrying two small bags. One contained medicines, the other contained her jewelry that her Captain had bought for her.

Hastily, the family took a count and discovered young Alice was missing. Al dashed back in, awakened his cousin, and carried her to safety. Robert Kleberg and Al then ran into the smoky office and vault at the southwest corner and were able to toss some of the ranch records and papers to safety.

Once aroused, Alice ran to ring the bell in the commissary tower. Its tolling carried all the way to Kingsville, but there was no fire fighting equipment to come. Helplessly, the family, their guests, and the *Kineños* watched the magnificent home burn.

Sam Ragland tried to move the piano, but Mrs. King ordered him to stop. "Let nobody get hurt," she said. "We can build a new home. We can't replace a life."

The fire grew hotter. Flames leaped into the sky. Timbers collapsed and red sparks whirled in the super-heated winds. Fine antiques, valuable furnishings, treasures of a lifetime, whirled away with them.

The fire was in their faces, but the icy wind was at their backs. The family started to retreat to the commissary.

In her black dress Henrietta King stood like a pillar until someone suggested that she too should leave. With one little black bag in her hand, she turned and threw a kiss to the dying house then looked back no more.

It was the passing of an era.

She was nearly eighty years old. By this time she had seen so much, lost so much, gained so much, built and rebuilt, that very little daunted her.

To no one's surprise she began a new era. She set forth a condition for the building of the new house. "Build a house that anybody can walk in *in boots*."

The Standard Passes

Like the Phoenix rising from the ashes, the great house rose again under the direction of Robert Kleberg. The respect and esteem in which he held his mother-in-law is evidenced by the speed with which the architect was engaged, the plans drawn, and the house completed. It was his tribute to her and her unfailing hospitality over all the years. Since she had come to the King Ranch as a bride, she had never turned anyone away.

Architect Carlton Adams was commissioned to design the new headquarters. What he created was a blend of San Antonio Mission style with Mediterranean. It took two years and $250,000 to build. The amount necessary to build it today would be in the millions.

Because the ranch had been so often threatened in the past, Adams gave the new mansion the security of a fortress as strong as any castle that ever rose above a mountaintop in Europe. Indeed, its towers and crenelations, its archways and tiles made it more like a castle than any other building in America at that time. Constructed of dazzling white stucco and concrete, it was built on the site of the old wooden house.

A side view of the mansion shows the Mediterranean look with red tiles and grillades. Note the tile decoration above the door. The peacock on the porch is one of many that stroll the grounds.
(Author photo)

The mansion stands on the site of the old house that burned. King's cannons from the original blockhouse still guard the valley to the east. (Author photo)

It had twenty-five rooms, each with a fireplace, and nearly as many baths, a revolutionary convenience for that time. It had wide cool verandas where Henrietta could sit and entertain her grandchildren. The halls were blue slate and the floor of the grand salon was mesquite, cut on the ranch, polished, and pegged with ebony. Both surfaces were floors for men to walk on in boots. Its walls were decorated with murals of the Alamo and of the ranch's wildlife and livestock. The dining hall would seat fifty guests. Italian bronze balustrades ascended along the marble stairway.

The watchtower rose sixty feet above ground. From it, guards could see for miles around, and guests could see it rise before them as they approached from Kingsville. Passengers could see it from the windows of the train. One of the major purchases in the design were three twenty-foot stained glass windows that rose up the front of the tower.

They were made by Louis Comfort Tiffany at a cost of $80,000.

The front lawn was enlarged. Peacocks strolled about it displaying their elegant feathers. Captain King's cannons from the old fort were rolled up to stand guard overlooking the Santa Gertrudis Creek toward the east. A patio was built with tropical trees and shrubs all blossoming with vivid flowers.

In the library—the repository of all the records that survived the fire and all the records to be added as the years rolled on—a mural of a tree was painted. The names of the Captain and his lady were painted at the root. All their children and grandchildren were depicted as the branches. Plenty of space was left for their descendants yet to come. The tree selected to bear their names was not the popular oak or apple, but a tree that had come to the Santa Gertrudis about the same time the Kings and Klebergs had come—the ubiquitous mesquite—tough and seemingly immortal.

The house was completed in 1914 and the family held two weddings there in 1915. Alice Gertrudis Kleberg married Tom East from Corpus Christi. Her older sister Henrietta Rosa married John Adrian Larkin of New York.

~ ~ ~

While life on the King Ranch continued steadily and peacefully, the world beyond its fences was becoming a dangerous place to live. In 1913 despite U.S. troops stationed all along the Mexican border, as well as four companies of the Texas militia and eight Texas Rangers in Brownsville, the problems with Mexico increased to the point where they could no longer be ignored.

Porfirio Diáz's famous *Rurales* were pulled back to the capital to protect his successor Madero. The revolution, simmering since Diáz's regime, now boiled over. Refugees poured across the border into Texas. Unless the poor souls were returned, rabidly anti-American Mexican rebels threatened to retaliate.

By 1914 the revolutionaries were abusing Americans at will. As in other wars, the Rio Grande was too far away from Washington for the U.S. president to worry about. All Woodrow Wilson's energies were concentrated on avoiding a war in Europe.

German agents, however, found Texas strategically perfect as well as a fertile ground for nefarious schemes. The Kaiser quickly sent army officers to teach military science and tactics to any squadron of armed troops they could contact in Mexico.

Raids across the border happened more often and became more destructive. Memories of King and Kenedy and their steamboats that had carried so much gold into Tamaulipas coffers were forgotten when German propaganda stirred old hatreds to remember San Jacinto and Buena Vista. Texans were shocked and frightened by the hostile attitudes of people they considered their good neighbors and trading partners.

In August 1915 a band of fifty Mexican horsemen rode north onto the King Ranch. The foreman at El Sauz alerted Caesar Kleberg, who telephoned from the new King ranch house for reinforcements to be sent from Brownsville. At the same time he started preparations at Kingsville. Within hours a train with a squad of troopers, some Texas Rangers, and several local peace officers arrived at Norias from Cameron County. There the Rangers and peace officers mounted Santa Gertrudis horses and rode southeast toward the El Sauz.

A few hours later the *bandidos* slipped by them to raid Norias. Armed with German Mauser rifles, they opened fire on the house. Two of the troopers and one visitor were hit immediately. As fast as they could grab their guns, the Texans fired back. The attackers took cover behind a pile of cross ties as well as other buildings in the yard.

The cook ran for the telephone on the ranch house porch. With bullets thudding into the walls around him, he rang Kingsville. "Mister Caesar!" he screamed. "We need help NOW!"

Caesar yelled that a train with men and guns was ready to roll out of Kingsville, but he couldn't find an engineer. If he didn't find one soon, he swore he would drive it himself.

Encouraged by the promise of reinforcements and rescue, the defenders fought on through the night. At dawn, the men who had gone to El Sauz returned, and shortly afterward two trains, one from Brownsville and one from Kingsville, arrived with not only reinforcements and ammunition but doctors and nurses as well.

A wounded *bandido* talked before he died. They were fools. They had not expected to find resistance, but he should have believed what his father had told him. The Texans were still *los diablos Tejanos*.

The raiders had planned to rob the ranch, the ranch store, and the southbound train. Then they were going to burn the house and the train. "The devil Texans" had held out too long.

Within the next six months, the King Ranch was raided twenty-six times by Mexican rebels. Isolated ranches belonging to other South Texans were terrorized. Trains were derailed and the wrecks robbed.

One night *bandidos* surrounded Alice Kleberg East near the corral of the ranch house at the King Ranch division of San Antonio Viejo. They wouldn't harm her, the leader said, if she would give them food. She was held in the ranch house while they took money, clothing, groceries, and horses. Neither did they burn the ranch house as they had done other people's homes in the area. Undoubtedly, they had sense enough to fear reprisals if a princess of the Santa Gertrudis was harmed.

South Texas had become an armed camp. Except for the *Kineños*, every Mexican posed a possible threat to every Anglo. All during the troubled times, the loyalty of the King people was never questioned. They manned the watchtowers taking care of Henrietta and her children, her many grandchildren, and now her great-grandchildren. No one was ever foolish enough to try to raid the new great house.

ᘁ ᘁ ᘁ

During 1916 Robert Kleberg suffered a stroke. It left him palsied and infirm in his mind. Though he remained the nominal head of the ranch and as such still ordered himself to be taken for drives every day across its ranges, he could no longer conduct its business.

His oldest son, Dick, had suffered a ruptured appendix that nearly killed him. His recovery took many months. When he did recover, his Texas Ranger commission and his perfect command of both English and Spanish kept him on duty with Army Intelligence on the border.

The mantle of *El Señor Capitán* fell to Robert Justus Kleberg Jr., just twenty-one years old and the third of that name. When his draft number came up the next year, his father filed an appeal for his deferment. When it was granted, he and his brother were branded draft dodgers with enemy sympathies. For the rest of his life he suffered from the slurs of local Anglos whose sons went off to war.

Bob Kleberg never served in the armed services, but for the rest of his life, he managed his *Kineños* as ably as any general on any battlefield.

More like his grandfather Richard King than anyone else, he gave all his energy and all his talent to the ranch.

From the minute he took command, he drove stripped-down cars at breakneck speeds across its broad expanses. Where the cars could not go, he rode the strong horses that he loved. He had a vision for the ranch, and he had strength of will to build the ranch so that others could see it.

His grandmother loved him. A photograph of them together shows him posing with a twelve-point buck that he shot. His arm is around her neck and she is holding onto his hand. Surely, she saw in him the rebirth of her Captain when she heard his great plans for the ranch.

One of his first decisions was to hire J. K. Northway, a young Doctor of Veterinary Medicine, fresh from college. His job was to begin breeding programs that would develop better herds of cattle and horses to work the cattle. The longhorn was an anachronism and the shorthorn was unsuited to the Texas climate. It could not hold its own against the problems of drought, screwworms, ear ticks, and fever ticks.

Northway set to work immediately. Using the shorthorns as his base, he crossed them with the Brahman or Zebu, the sacred cattle of India. He obtained these cattle from A. P. Borden's herd near Galveston.

Their arrival caused consternation. They were taller and rangier than shorthorns or longhorns. When Alice Gertrudis Kleberg first saw them, she noted that they didn't look as if they would provide as much meat as a longhorn. Their brindle and smoky gray hides with their black faces and knees were dirty looking. She told her son that she didn't like them. She "hated to see the red cattle go."

Fortunately, her objections were overruled because the new imported cattle looked so promising. The Brahmans were shorthaired, hearty, fast growing, and indifferent to summer heat. Unfortunately, as Alice had recognized instantly, they did not make any more meat than a longhorn. Perhaps when they were bred to a shorthorn, something with greater potential might emerge. A breeding program began immediately.

About this same time Caesar Kleberg bought a young stallion from a neighboring rancher for $125. Almost the moment the animal was unloaded on the ranch his unusually fine conformation and his intelligence became apparent. Indeed, he was broken and put to work too fast for someone to give him a proper name. All his life he was called simply Old Sorrel.

In time he changed the character and quality of the Santa Gertrudis horse stock. Indirectly and directly, he influenced all horses used for herding cattle over much of the United States.

He was a grandson of Peter McCue and a son of Hickory Bill, both prominent quarter horse stallions. His dam was a Kentucky mare whose background contained considerable Thoroughbred blood. Bob Kleberg's determination and generalship is exemplified by the fact that even with continued raids (twenty-six in that year) from south of the border, the real work of the Santa Gertrudis accelerated. They never once faltered in their effort to perfect breeds of horses and cattle.

ꟽ ꟽ ꟽ

In 1917 when the U.S. entered World War I, the crackpot plan that had fueled all the raiding, all the thieving, all the destruction, and all the useless bloodshed was revealed. Germany had been in negotiations with Mexico and Japan to declare war on the United States. They were to keep America occupied on her own continent and out of the war in Europe.

According to the "Plan of San Diego," when Germany had conquered all of Europe, she would come to the aid of her allies in a mopping-up operation. While Germany brought the United States of America under the Kaiser's rule, the Southwest would be restored to Mexico and the Northwest would be given to Japan.

One can only speculate what would have happened if the Santa Gertrudis had not lain like a bastion across the Wild Horse Desert from the Rio Grande to the Nueces. Had the men at Norias not been willing fight, to hold out though heavily outnumbered with ammunition running low, the success of that first bandit raid would have encouraged others.

The Norias Rangers of 1918. These men were among the many who defended the King Ranch and simultaneously the American border during World War I. (Courtesy of the Texas and Southwestern Cattle Raisers Foundation, Fort Worth, Texas)

More Germans could have been landed at Matamoros. Indeed an army as well as a steady stream of supplies could have been brought to the back door of the United States much as King and Kenedy had carried cotton out the back door during the Civil War.

Germany never stood a chance.

The Klebergs, only four generations removed from Germany, fought with guns and trains and telephones and all the technology that their enterprise could utilize. Beside them fought the *Kineños*, only three generations removed from the lost town of Cruillas, Tamaulipas.

Did they think they were defending America? Probably not. What they knew was that they were fighting for the place they had carved for themselves. They were fighting for the Santa Gertrudis—for the King Ranch. It was their home and the home of their families and their livelihood. In the end that is the reason all men fight.

And in the end it is enough.

The Myth

The Ghost's Diamond

U.S. Highway 77 lies arrow straight. Its two parallel tracks of concrete bisect the King Ranch like knife cuts. With never a bend or a curve, it stretches between Kingsville in Kleberg County through Kenedy County to Raymondville in Willacy County. For seventy-two miles a car can run seventy miles an hour, slowed by only one town, a wide place in the road called Riviera and a border patrol checkpoint.

Of course, few people care to drive only seventy miles an hour.

Today, the highway is a divided four-lane, but once it was a sea of grass, then a cow path, then a pair of stagecoach ruts, then a gravel road, and then a narrow two-lane highway. Very narrow with no shoulders and thickets of nearly impenetrable *brasada* on either side.

The night was cool. The prevailing breeze swept across the thirty-some-odd miles from the Gulf of Mexico, swept across sand dunes, swept through mesquite and cactus *brasada*, swept past grazing Santa Gertrudis cattle, dozing saddle horses, and sleeping *Kineños* rolled up in their bedrolls in the cow camps.

It swept in through the open window of the big white Fleetwood Cadillac V16.

He had bought it five years before in 1940 just before World War II. It was a monster of a car, admirably suited to make the drive through the King Ranch. Its great size and power allowed it to roar easily over the roads at a hundred miles an hour. It out-drove its own headlights by hundreds of feet.

He had tuned his radio to Del Rio, Texas, where a genuine autographed picture of Jesus Christ could be purchased for only nine-ninety-nine. The music was Mexican mariachi and American jitterbug. It suited him.

So did his big Cuban cigar. He puffed on it energetically and occasionally patted the wheel in time to the blaring notes.

His left arm was cocked out the window. His hand, holding the big cigar, did not touch the wheel. Who needed to steer when the Cadillac held the road so well? And the road was ramrod straight.

On his little finger he wore a diamond ring, two and a half carats in a brilliant cut, set in eighteen-carat yellow gold. The symbol of his success. In fact, all of them were symbols of his success—the cigar and the nonchalance with which he smoked it, the Cadillac and the speed at which he drove it.

He smiled as he drove. He saw the headlights coming toward him. High and wide—a truck. He didn't slow. He didn't twist his wheel and move as close as he could to the side of the narrow highway.

High, wide, and handsome, he sped toward the looming lights.

He had no time to react. His speed met the speed of the truck in a vicious sideswipe. The impact took the Cadillac's front fender, its searchlight, its mirror, its doors, and his left arm.

The car's speed and power carried it on down the highway nearly a quarter of a mile before he could get it stopped. Only then did he realize blood was spouting from his shoulder. It couldn't be. He felt no pain. He could still smell the smoke of his cigar. He could still feel the vibration of the powerful engine as with his right hand he reached down to turn off the ignition.

With failing sight, he slumped back against the blood-soaked seat and watched his world go black.

ꟿ ꟿ ꟿ

They buried him without his arm. His wife and children were inconsolable. Their grief was a pitiful thing to watch. His friends remembered him as a good man. Privately, they shook their heads as they envisioned some coyote or bobcat making a meal off his arm.

Several weeks passed before anyone remembered the diamond ring. The site of the wreck was known. A mile and a half north of the Norias loading pens. It was the description the highway patrol had radioed when they'd come upon the wreck. Moreover, his wife had marked the spot with a flowery cross, staked just where he'd brought the Cadillac to a stop, the spot where he'd bled to death.

ꟿ ꟿ ꟿ

How much trouble could it be to pull up in a pickup and climb through the wire?

Three of his acquaintances drove up the road from Raymondville at sunrise. Walking along the road scrutinizing the shoulder, they found what they were sure was the exact spot where the collision had taken place. A small line of slivers of glass and metal remained where the wrecker crew had swept up the last of the debris.

The sky turned from pink-streaked gray to blue. The sun burst over the horizon.

The three men looked hard in both directions. Nobody and nothing stirred in the Wild Horse Desert. Then they crawled between the top strands of barbed wire and the King Ranch net onto the pathway worn bare by trailing cattle and fence riders.

The sweat trickled down their faces and wet their shirts between their shoulder blades. They were trespassing and they knew the chance they were taking. The *Kineños* who patrolled the pastures all carried rifles on their saddles. Most strapped pistols to their hips as well.

The men knew they could be shot and their bodies left to rot where they fell or dragged farther into the brush and summarily shoveled under. But the diamond was two and a half carats. Worth a lot of money. Even split three ways.

They reasoned that the truck had thrown his arm north, so with eyes and noses trained, they walked up the trail. A man's whole arm was a pretty big thing, longer than a yard. It might be more than a coyote would want to drag off. He might just leave it where it lay.

When they'd gone nearly half a mile without seeing or smelling anything, they knew they had to leave the trail and trace the way back through the *brasada*.

One of them was for giving up entirely. The sun that had risen so brightly was now dimming as gray clouds boiled in from the Gulf. The wind freshened and tugged at their sweat-stained hats. The air, heavy with moisture, intensified the smell of creosote. It seemed to press around them.

They agreed to walk twenty feet apart back in a straight line. If they didn't find anything, they'd come back another day with a dog. Maybe an animal could sniff out something. They didn't discuss this idea, but the thoughts of a coon hound finding a man's arm gave them all the chills.

The most eager agreed to go the farthest in. The least enthusiastic stepped off ten feet from the path. He stood and watched as the other two left him. When they had gone far enough, he could see only part of the blue shirt his friend was wearing through the tangles of brush.

The other went on and disappeared completely. Fifty feet into the King Ranch, the mesquite and cactus grew too thick to see through. The man closest to the fence wished he were anywhere else but there. The cool breeze was drying the perspiration on his shirt. He shivered.

Judging that it was time to make the move, he started ahead, looking from right to left, peering under the brush on both sides, keeping his eyes peeled.

From time to time he straightened up. Both of his friends had disappeared completely. He patted the keys to the pickup. He thought about leaving the search right now and going back across the fence. He didn't have to tell them what he'd done. He'd just be standing there when they came out. He wasn't going to find anything. Nobody was going to find anything. No one would get lost. No one would get shot.

At that thought he shook his head and scowled. What had made him think such a thing? They were all going to come through this just fine. Nobody was going to shoot them. Those days were gone forever. If someone should come by, they'd just be ordered off with a warning.

Lightning flashed out of a heavy gray cloud in the west. The squall was coming fast. He made his way along more smartly now. The mesquites shivered and whipped from the wind. One slashed him in the face as he bent to look beneath it. He didn't believe in ghosts.

What had put that thought into his head?

He looked behind him. He couldn't help it. Nothing. He couldn't see anything in front of him either, nor to either side. He was completely surrounded by the brush. He was only ten feet off the trail, only thirty off the highway, but he might have been a hundred.

He ducked low to miss the spreading limb of a big mesquite, took a step forward, and stumbled over a root. He stared at the thing. Somehow the gray gnarled wood had poked up above the ground to catch the toe of his boot. He'd have to be more careful. He watched where he put his foot, but somehow when he took his next step, he fell forward sprawling. The inch-long thorns of a whippy little huisache grazed his cheek.

The blood trickled hot. He clapped his hand to his cheek and lay there cursing. Thunder rumbled closer. The sky was gray overhead. He was wasting his time. They were all wasting their time. They weren't going to find anything.

He started to push himself to his feet. Then right under his nose he saw half a Cuban cigar. The gold band was still around it.

He began to shake. The wind whipped the mesquite limbs above his head. The bitter green huisache slashed at his eyes. The thunder sounded closer. The first drops of rain began to fall. The arm of the dead man must be near. If the cigar was on the ground under his nose, the diamond ring must be right around here close.

He reached out his hand—surprised to see that it trembled.

He couldn't bring himself to touch the thing.

Lightning flashed, turning the day white. Thunder boomed in almost the same instant. Huge drops of rain struck his head, his back. He jumped to his feet. He could smell the ozone, smell the creosote, smell—the cigar. He could smell the cigar smoke. The smoke in the rain.

And flesh. He could smell rotting flesh. In the rain.

The lightning flashed again. Every twisted gray limb turned white. Every mesquite frond swirled. He screamed, but he couldn't hear his own voice above the thunder.

He ran! Bolted through the *brasada*. The thorns tore his Levis, scratched his face and arms. He jerked and twisted around. He screeched as they clawed at him. He couldn't find the path. He blundered back and forth. He was running in a circle.

Sobbing, he collided with his fellow searchers. They clasped each other's shoulders and stared while the rain beat down on their heads. He was glad the rain was hitting him. His friends wouldn't know he was crying. It was bad enough they knew he chickened out and ran.

No one said a word as they turned themselves due west with their backs to the storm and ran. Somehow when they broke out onto the path, the storm had passed. The rain had stopped as suddenly as it began. The thunder faded to a distant rumble. The sky turned blue again.

Shamefaced, they climbed back between the barbed wire and the King Ranch net. Silently, they walked down the highway to the pickup.

While the other two were climbing in, he collapsed against the side of the pickup. Bending over, he dragged in great gulps of hot, humid air.

The air smelled of rain and creosote and not the least bit like a Cuban cigar.

Part VI

"The Walled Kingdom of Texas"

The Truth

The Blood of Champions

Throughout World War I, Dr. Northway continued to develop the breeding program. He was convinced that a meat-producing cow was essential, but all of the existent breeds of such cattle were bred to do well in temperate climates.

For example the cousins of the shorthorn, the English Herefords, were particularly unsuitable for the Wild Horse Desert. Their curly hair made a perfect place for ticks to hide and grow. Screwworms laid their eggs in the sores left by the ticks. The distinctive white faces had no pigment in the skin beneath the snowy white hair. The fierce sunlight burned cancers on their eyelids that eventually caused them to lose their eyes.

Northway was convinced Brahmans were the answer. He planned that many animals were to be bred in many different combinations.

Bob Kleberg himself selected the animals for breeding. From sunup to sundown, until Northway and all the cowpunchers were exhausted, he stood at the side of the cattle chutes inspecting as many as a thousand heifers in a day and sometimes selecting as few as six to be bred.

The purpose of all this mixing and matching—as it is in all breeding programs—was to produce the perfect individual. Problems arise because one can never tell which newborn calf will turn out to be perfect.

A Brahman bull named Vinotero was mated to a shorthorn cow on the Laureles grant. She was blood red in color and herself one-sixteenth Brahman. The result was a bull calf that must not have looked like much when he was born. He was given the unprepossessing name of Monkey and pretty much forgotten. In fact, he was exhibited at the State Fair of Texas in 1921 as a yearling and almost sold there with the lot.

To say that he was an accident, however, is to misspeak. He was the result of carefully planned breeding. His appearance was the result of exactly the right mix of genetic material. Other bulls and cows of his generation were also fine, but he was exceptional.

Later, Bob and Dick Kleberg both claimed responsibility for spotting him and recognizing his potential and bringing the bull back to the ranch for the breeding program. Ranch foremen and animal trainers, including the famous Librado Maldonado Sr., also claimed they picked him out. No one really knows. The fact is that they did.

Monkey was an amazing animal. His dark cherry red hide became the trademark of the Santa Gertrudis breed. He turned out to be not only the best individual ever seen on the Santa Gertrudis, but his characteristics were so potent that his offspring, both male and female, bred true. From him came an astonishing parade of dark cherry red cattle. A photograph of four of his sons taken side by side has the look of four cardboard cutouts, so identical in size and conformation are they.

Breeding true, however, would not have been the real test. He and his progeny had to prove they could survive and

Monkey, the progenitor of the Santa Gertrudis breed.
(Courtesy of the Texas and Southwestern Cattle Raisers Foundation, Fort Worth, Texas)

prosper in the Wild Horse Desert. And so they did. Like the Brahman, they had the remarkable ability to rustle for their food under the blazing sun in humidity and drought. Like the shorthorn they gained weight in a heavier, deeper meat-making conformation that meant larger production of desirable cuts for the butcher shop. The hide was a distinctive color, almost unique in the world at that time. Its dark red came from a blend of Brahman and shorthorn pigmentation, which resisted burning and shrugged off flies and ticks.

Northway practiced line breeding and close inbreeding so that the entire herd for many years was directly descended from Monkey. The bull was first mated to first-cross and double-cross heifers all carefully selected for their conformation, all cherry red in color. From them came matings to the best of his granddaughters. Likewise, the best of his sons were mated to the daughters that best complemented them. Staying with the one family and using both males and females to correct any problematical characteristics produced a steady improvement in the breed.

The beautiful cattle prospered on the Santa Gertrudis, the Laureles, the Encino, and the Norias. The result was the cattle soon were desired by every serious rancher worldwide in the tropic zones.

Bob Kleberg, looking over the pastures dotted with the new cows, could say to his mother with pride and affection, "Well, Mother, you got your red cattle back."

ʍ ʍ ʍ

Bob and Caesar Kleberg were equally excited about the colts of Old Sorrel, the quarter horse stallion Caesar had bought for $125. By coincidence or design he was a red horse, a lighter color than Monkey, but red nevertheless. To this day the King Ranch raises and trains red animals.

Once Old Sorrel was broken and tried for cattle work, he proved to be far and away the best cow horse the ranch had ever seen. He was beautiful, his disposition was sweet. His conformation was perfect for his job. And his smoothness of action and his ability to work cattle were uncanny. He had real intelligence and a flair for the work.

Old Sorrel's breed was the quarter horse, so-called because of his ability to run "like his tail was on fire" for a quarter of a mile. The horse was an ideal pony for working stock, for playing polo, for hunting, and for everyday riding.

He had heavy-muscled hind legs and hindquarters from which came his exceptional power. His back was excellent for the saddle. It allowed the rider to sit just behind the shoulder. His flexible neck was long and extended forward with the heavy head dropping down at the end. It did not fit the heroic mold for English gentry and European generals. Yet this conformation gave the horse its ability to twist and turn. The cowboys sang that he "could turn on a nickel and give you the change."

Such a horse was Old Sorrel. When his talents were known, he was bred to fifty of the best handling and best riding mares on the Santa Gertrudis. They were in most cases pure Thoroughbred or grade Thoroughbred breeders. The best horse colt from the result was Solis, who was then bred back to his half sisters.

The system that had worked with Monkey and his progeny produced one of the finest and most famous lines of quarter horses anywhere in the world. The prime result of the exceptional breeding was a stallion named Peppy, a double grandson of Old Sorrel, who in turn sired Mr. San Peppy and his son Peppy San Badger, both retired and living on the King Ranch today.

The breeding of these animals was necessary to produce the numbers of mounts with exceptional stamina and skill to work the ranch. The Santa Gertrudis wanted only the best. Their training was far different from the horrible experience that had "broken" horses throughout the western United States and Mexico for generations.

Because Bob and Caesar Kleberg loved horses, they deplored bronc-busting. They made sure that the practice, which included letting a horse run wild on the range until it was three or four years old and then being brutally broken by main force, would never be done on the Santa Gertrudis. Their horses were kept close and handled constantly.

The practice of halter-breaking the colts is an example of the gentle method that they instituted. The King Ranch keeps a herd of *burros*, beasts known for their placid temperaments. When the colts are weaned from their mothers, they are turned into the pasture with the little creatures.

For four hours a day every day, they are haltered and tied by foot-long lines to the halters on the burros. Wherever the

The King Ranch burros graze alone in the late summer.
Every spring they work to halter break the new colts.
(Author photo)

burros go, the colts must follow right alongside. When the burros graze, the colts must drop their heads and graze too. If the colts try to fight the line, the burros stubbornly sit down.

Within weeks the colts are trained to follow wherever the pressure on the halter takes them.

The King Ranch no longer maintains so many animals as it once did. In Old Sorrel's time sixteen to seventeen horses trained in this manner were issued to every *vaquero*. The animals were trained by their rider and ridden by him in accordance with the established practices of the ranch.

Today with pickups carrying the men all around the ranch, a man needs only six or seven horses on his string to do the actual rounding up. The cow camps too are a thing of the past because the pickups carry the men back home at night.

ʬ ʬ ʬ

Henrietta King did not live to see the magnificent herds of red cattle herded by her stalwart *Kineños* atop sorrel, chestnut, and bay quarter horses. Like anyone else who lives to the great age of ninety-two, she knew herself to be the last leaf, the survivor of an age forever in the past. She had made her will in 1918, a twenty-two-page document that provided for everyone and at the same time forbade the dissolution of the ranch.

It was the last thing she could do to carry out the trust her Captain had handed to her. The Santa Gertrudis Ranch, the King's ranch, indivisible and indissoluble, would go on after her death in so far as she was able to preserve it.

At the Santa Gertrudis ranch house, she died about ten o'clock in the evening, March 21, 1925.

The news of her death brought the convergence of a far-flung family. Of her five children only her daughter Alice had outlived her. But her death brought her grandchildren to her side and her great-grandchildren. Friends and acquaintances came to pay their respects. The rich and powerful came to acknowledge the passing of one of their very own as well as to respect the powerful grandsons who were even now gazing hawk-eyed around them.

Most poignant was the convergence of the *Kineños*. From the farthest corners of the South Texas pastures, they came with their wide-brimmed hats in their hands. Their wives came with them and their children. They parked their wagons and their cars on the grass under the trees.

The foremen of the cow camps presented themselves at headquarters to their new *patrona*, Alice Gertrudis King Kleberg, in the ancient feudal style, to express their sorrow formally and to pledge their faithfulness to her family.

The honor guard from the house to the cemetery in Kingsville was a procession of two hundred mounted men in their range clothes. At the cemetery during the hymns, eulogies, and prayers, Manhattan bankers in Brooks Brothers suits rubbed shoulders with Levi Strauss denim worn by *vaqueros* from El Sauz and Norias.

After the coffin was lowered into the earth, each of the *vaqueros* mounted and rode his horse in a dash around the grave, their hats down at their sides in salute. The dust that rose and fell on the coffin was a far more tender farewell than the clods that fell after they rode away in silence.

That autumn the remains of her daughter Ella, her son Lee, and of her Captain were brought from San Antonio and reinterred by her side. They sleep together there under a tall granite shaft incised with the single word KING.

ʷ ʷ ʷ

Henrietta King had prepared for her death and had left everything as it should be, as she had said she would. Eight trustees were named originally. Five were old men, one of whom had predeceased her. The other three were her grandsons Richard King III, Richard Mifflin Kleberg, and Robert J. Kleberg Jr. Like their grandfather before them, they were eager to take the helm of the greatest ranch in the world.

An appraisal of the ranch reckoned its assets at seven million dollars. As when the Captain had died, the debts were there too. It had more than a million and a half in liabilities. The debts were as worrisome as they had been in King's day with the added problems of having to raise the cash to pay the huge estate taxes.

Again the King Ranch faced an uncertain future, for added to the debt was the will's stipulation that the estate was not to be settled for ten years. All the heirs would have to wait until 1935 to receive their shares. James Wells, with his clever head for business, had advised Mrs. King to make this provision to forestall large portions of the ranch having to be sold so each could have a share.

The ten-year respite was just what Bob Kleberg needed. He used the time to establish a position of strength for the ranch. He was to need all that strength since he seemed to step naturally into the role of heir apparent. While Richard King and Dick Kleberg pursued other interests, he became the guiding force as his father and grandfather had before him and the custodian of the Kleberg's future plans.

In 1926 he took time out to get married. As in everything he did all his life long, he ran at marriage with the speed of a bolting quarter horse. In the middle of February, he went to San Antonio on business. That evening he was introduced to Helen Campbell, the daughter of the Honorable Philip Pitt Campbell, Congressman from Kansas. She was beautiful, she was educated, she lived in Washington, D.C., she had toured Europe. He had dropped out of college after two years to devote his whole life and thought to the South Texas ranch.

Seventeen days later, on March 2, they married in Corpus Christi. After a ten-day wedding trip to New York, they hurried back to the Santa Gertrudis.

As opposite as they were, they were great friends as well as very much in love. She was always interested in his work and traveled with him frequently. Still clashes arose out of their disparate backgrounds.

For example, she had an Easterner's love of Thoroughbred horses and a distinct prejudice in their favor. Bob always maintained that a good working animal could do just about anything it was asked to do whether it was bred for it or not.

Once when Helen Kleberg was training her Thoroughbreds to jump the course she had constructed, Bob made some disparaging comments about their long legs and long thin bodies. She rose to their defense, saying that their conformation was necessary to make the high jumps.

With a shrug Bob had Old Sorrel brought out to the course. He led the stallion around it. Then he mounted, bareback with no bit in the animal's mouth, and took the horse over the jumps in perfect order.

Helen was astonished that the heavier animal had so easily disproved her statement, but Bob just grinned. He'd made his point. He was one of the first influential people to recognize the general overall excellence of the American Quarter Horse.

The ease with which Bob won his woman gave him confidence that he could take the Santa Gertrudis out of debt.

ꟺ ꟺ ꟺ

The Humble Oil & Refining Company of Houston had leased land and explored for oil before Henrietta's death. No oil had been found although there had been indications aplenty of mineral wealth. Now Bob suggested to the Humble executives that they mount a careful reconsideration of the oil potential.

He mentioned that he doubted if oilmen could show him any million acres along the Gulf Coast between Louisiana and Tampico, Mexico, where oil was not present. If the Humble company would obligate itself to explore and develop the minerals and to make annual bonus payments large enough to cover the interest on the debts owed by the estate, the company could have exclusive drilling rights to that particular million acres.

Nearly eight years after Henrietta's death, Humble leased the lands of her heirs, the acreages of which Bob Kleberg was trustee, and the Santa Gertrudis headquarters tract, which had been left exclusively to his mother. In all the company leased 1,133,156.31 acres for which the ranch received the first cash payment of $3,223,645. The sum was enough to clear away the debt.

Though oil discovery was not immediately forthcoming, Humble eased the King Ranch's burden and allowed the ranching business experiments to continue.

King Ranch, Incorporated

The tremendous expense of ridding the ranch of cattle ticks finally paid off in 1928. The final phase of the United States Department of Agriculture's long campaign ended in victory. The monetary cost of the long battle is unknown. A partial list of expenses includes twenty-four dipping vats built on ranch property; the chemical solutions for the vats; hundreds of miles of barbed wire fence replaced by higher, heavier, stronger, tighter wire; and the pay for extra hands required to round up, herd, dip, and redip the cattle as well as patrol every mile of ranch to be sure infected cattle did not stray into cleaned pastures.

When Robert J. Kleberg Sr. began the program in 1889, he had known it would be expensive. Yet, even he could not have counted such an outlay to have southmost Texas declared tick free. Only the greatest ranch in the world could have launched such a program and sustained it for the thirty-nine years it took to declare the ranch tick free.

Along with the eradication of the ticks, the ranch had launched a program to improve the grass. African Rhodes grass seemed perfect for Texas soil and weather. It was imported and planted over 17,000 acres. It grew so well it was harvested for hay and select cattle were turned in after the harvest for choice grazing. The dream of agriculture on King Ranch had become something perhaps more valuable—pasture improvement.

Eventually the Rhodes grass was found to be susceptible to a scale-creating insect that somehow had made its way from Japan, perhaps in a packing case of chinaware. With the swiftness of the plague, the Rhodes grass as well as native grasses succumbed.

Bob Kleberg called the Texas Agriculture and Mechanical University Experiment Station. Too late to save the Rhodes grass, but soon enough to save the rest of the coastal plain, the university located a microscopic wasp that had been imported from the Far East to Hawaii to combat the same scale in the sugarcane. It was imported and the cattle industry in Texas was saved.

The near disaster convinced Bob Kleberg of the necessity for new types of grass to be constantly in development. Over the years the King Ranch has developed its own King Ranch blue stem, bristle-joint blue stem, Caesar grass, coastal Bermuda, and giant Bermuda. In fact, more than a dozen different types of grass grow on the King Ranch. If one develops problems and dies off, the others quickly rush in to cover the barren ground.

Another momentous discovery had to do with grass. Bob Kleberg imported a small herd of Africander cattle from the Union of South Africa. His original plan was to use them to improve his own breeding program. That he did not use them is unimportant. What was important is what he learned from them.

In the dry areas of Africa, cattle were periodically given a spoonful of phosphorus-bearing chemical to make them fatten more readily. If they put on more weight, they must be in better health. An analysis of the native grasses of the Santa Gertrudis found them phosphorus-deficient because the soil lacked the mineral in times of drought. The reason for the low weight of cows in some particular pastures as well as the appearance of arthritis in those cows as the deficiency became more pronounced was therefore explained. Lack of phosphorus was causing their poor bone development.

The addition of phosphorus to salt licks and drinking water brought the weight back on the cattle. Calf production in dry years jumped over thirty percent.

Bob Kleberg's discovery was detailed in *The Cattleman* in 1947. Its effect worldwide cannot be overestimated. Millions of acres which had heretofore been unusable for unknown reasons now were opened to moneymaking beef production. The beef raised on these acres provided protein in the fight against world hunger.

ꟿ ꟿ ꟿ

While Bob and Helen Kleberg labored to build the ranch, Dick Kleberg rode off in another direction. In November 1931 the Republican incumbent of the 14th Congressional District died. Dick ran against the Republican nominee. Using the Democratic platform of States' Rights with less government interference, Dick won. His seat helped John Nance Garner from Uvalde, Texas, to become Speaker of the House from which he was chosen by Franklin Delano Roosevelt to be his vice-president.

The following year Robert Justus Kleberg, the man Captain King had hand picked to be the husband of Alice Gertrudis, died in his upstairs room on the Santa Gertrudis. His family was beside him. The *Kineños* marked the passing of *El Abogado* as they had *La Patrona*. In 1932 the Captain's ranch well and truly passed into the hands of his descendants.

The next year the Klebergs negotiated for the purchase of the interests from the heirs of Ella and Nettie. And in

1934 Alice Kleberg and her two sons organized a family corporation. The stockholders, consisting entirely of the family, put their shares in a trust administered by the Kleberg brothers. Richard Sr. was elected chairman of the board. Bob became president and general manager.

Robert Justus Kleberg Jr., President and General Manager of King Ranch, Inc.

ʬ ʬ ʬ

After nearly eighty years the Santa Gertrudis Ranch ceased to exist as the overall name for the boundless acres. It officially named itself what it had been called for almost that entire time—King Ranch.

The heirs of Henrietta King at last received their inheritance. Most of them were content to leave it where it lay under the name of King Ranch with Bob Kleberg as its general manager and chief operating officer. Those who disagreed or who brought costly suits against the corporation for partition found themselves spending a great deal of money. Indeed, they got little satisfaction and no more land than they were entitled to for all their trouble.

As if the Captain himself were looking after his ranch, the huge property remained largely intact and continued to prosper. For ease of management it was divided into four sections. The Santa Gertrudis with the ranch house as its headquarters comprised 203,468.19 acres. The Laureles, which had been bought from Mifflin Kenedy, comprised 255,026.53 acres. The Norias where Caesar Kleberg ruled was made up of 237,348.96, and the Encino, 131,348.07.

ᴡ ᴡ ᴡ

The Kleberg brothers must have felt supremely confident in 1936. Their debts were paid. The ranch they loved was safe for their lifetimes. They had beautiful, loving wives and exceptional children. One lived in Washington and Corpus Christi. The other lived in one of the most beautiful and famous houses in America. South on the Norias and the El Sauz, the Humble Oil and Refining Company, later to become Exxon, was drilling, drilling, drilling, determined to tap the rich field of oil and natural gas that their geologists told them lay below.

The time had come to have some fun.

In 1938 the brothers bought Kentucky Derby and Preakness winner Bold Venture. He was a magnificent sorrel. (Was his color the result of King Ranch bias for red animals?) He became the first important stud of their new stable. The *Kineños* approved immediately. He didn't look like a long-legged rangy Thoroughbred. He wasn't skittish and bad-tempered. He looked and acted like a real horse—a quarter horse.

His care and hands-on breeding were handled by Max Hirsch, who had trained him and who helped select the mares to mate with him to produce the best Thoroughbreds. With Hirsch as its head, the breeding program began with the idea that King Ranch would produce a line of champions. How Bob Kleberg's eyes gleamed as he watched those first beautiful long-legged colts frolicking on the green acres beside Santa Gertrudis Creek!

While they matured, he had much more to be proud of. The year 1940 saw probably the single most important event in the history of ranching in the Western Hemisphere. Indeed it turned out to be a momentous event worldwide. The United States Department of Agriculture, Bureau of Animal Industry, officially recognized the Santa Gertrudis as a new and separate breed of cattle, with its own characteristics as defined and firmly fixed as those of any other recognized breed.

Twenty years after Monkey's death, the careful line breeding and crossbreeding of the bull's progeny as it had been documented was acknowledged to be true. No longer would the big cherry red cattle be designated as a crossbreed—five parts shorthorn and three parts Brahman. They were themselves, a distinct breed whose characteristics would not produce throwbacks to their origins.

They would take their place in the world beside Aberdeen Angus and English Herefords, beside Guernseys, Jerseys, and Holsteins, beside Charolais, Limousin, and Simmental. The United States of America had at last produced a new breed of cattle, and it came from the King Ranch.

That same year the American Quarter Horse Association was formed for the purpose of declaring the quarter horse a true and separate breed different from any other breed in the world. In 1941 at the Southwestern Exposition and Fat Stock Show in Fort Worth, the Grand Champion Stallion of that year had the honor of being named first in the studbook. Wimpy, a double grandson of Old Sorrel, was the first recognized Quarter Horse in America.

Wimpy. Note the solid conformation of hindquarters, heavily muscled thighs, and wideset forelegs. This stallion was No. 1 in the American Quarter Horse Stud Book and a sire of many of the most powerful and popular horses in the world. (Courtesy of the Texas and Southwestern Cattle Raisers Foundation, Fort Worth, Texas.)

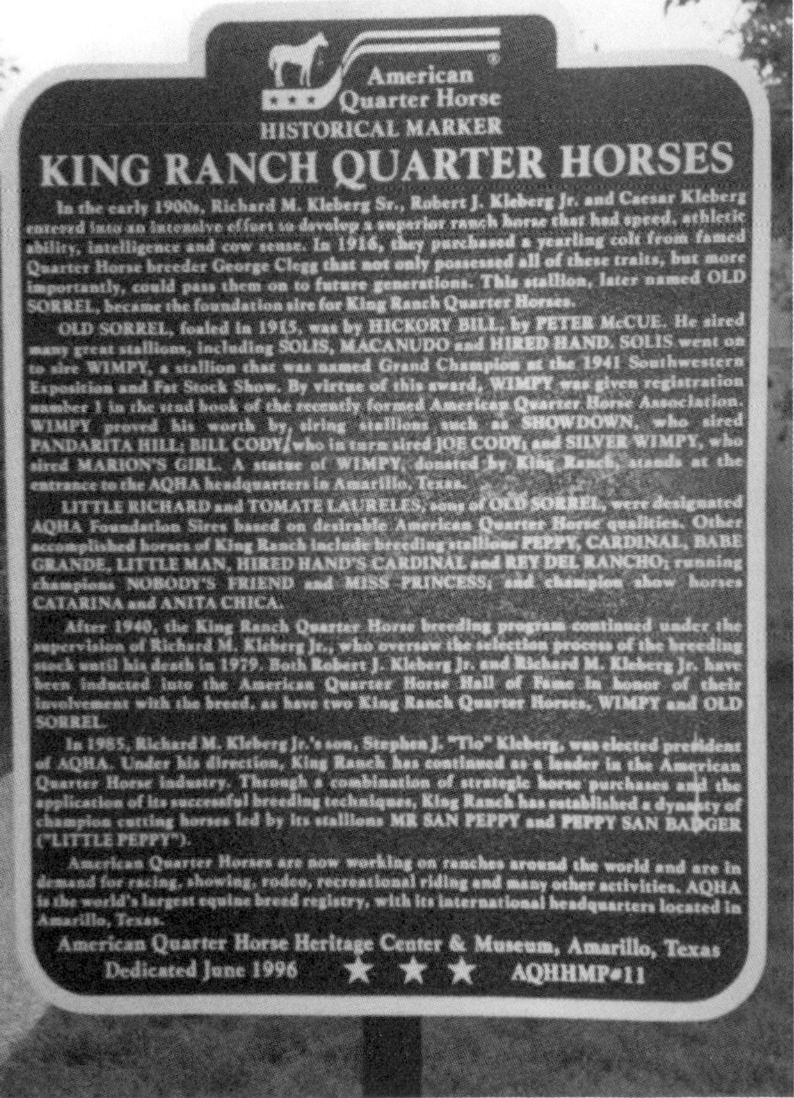

The historical marker erected by the American Quarter Horse Association describes the King Ranch's contributions to the development of the All-American horse. (Author photo.)

The King Ranch double triumph in two years was truly extraordinary. Yet Bob and Dick Kleberg probably felt something more like gratification and validation. They were fit heirs to the mantle of their grandfather. They were carrying on the tradition.

In 1945 Humble Oil drilled its first wildcat well on the King Ranch. In doing so the company discovered the Borregas Field, which was rated at that time the most important discovery in South Texas in eight years. Moreover, it lay entirely within the boundaries of the King Ranch.

A producing well. The rig or derrick has been dismantled and moved to another exploration site.
(From the Collections of the Texas/Dallas History and Archives Division, Dallas Public Library.)

The oil and gas royalties began rolling in. Though livestock sales were still the ranch's main source of income, the additional capital allowed the corporation to grow and expand much faster than it would have done. It allowed the Kleberg brothers to tackle projects with enthusiasm without counting the pennies required to bring them to fruition.

And more validation was yet to come. In 1943 Assault had been born. He was a big red chestnut, the son of Bold Venture out of Igual. His mother had a hard time birthing him. The question was raised as to whether both mare and colt were worth saving. Should the ranch have them destroyed to save expenses? Since money was no longer the prime consideration, the colt was named Assault and the pair was turned out to pasture.

Hard luck continued to plague the animal. The colt came in from the pasture limping. He had stepped on a surveyor's stake, which had split his hoof.

A horse's hoof is the equivalent of the third toenail of a person's foot. His leg to the knee is the third toe. The remains of what are his second and fourth toes grow as bony strips down the sides of the leg, which is called the cannon bone. The back of the knee or hock, which never touches the ground, is actually the horse's heel.

Inside the hoof is an elastic mass of tissue known as the frog. Assault had injured both his hoof and the frog it enclosed. Once the hoof is split and the frog scarred, the horse is usually finished. To expect him to race would be unthinkable.

But he was so valuable, so beautiful. Again there was money enough to work with him.

Lolo Treviño, a descendant of the De la Garza family from whom Captain King had bought the ranch, shaved away the fractured hoof and cleaned it. Dr. Northway applied ointment to the wound and bandaged it. Though it healed, it would never be the same.

Still Bob Kleberg couldn't bear to have him destroyed.

Juan Silva, a *Kineño* and blacksmith of the ranch, rebuilt the hoof. Dr. Northway designed a special shoe with a cushioned leather innersole to support the frog. Everybody laughed and called the horse "the slow-footed comet." He would never bring a return to the money invested in him.

But heart is everything in a horse and in a man. After his first gallop around the track, Assault was desperate to run. If the day was too wet, he would get nervous and excited. He would buck and pitch and bite. Only when a trainer or a jockey was up on his back would he settle down. Once out on the track, approaching the starting gate, his concentration was total. All his superb strength and mind and heart were leashed tight—until the time came to run.

Everyone on the ranch knew about him. He'd been entered in the greatest race in America. One man remembers how he and some other *vaqueros* were branding calves on the Laureles when Dick Kleberg drove up in his car. They turned on the radio and listened to the Kentucky Derby.

When Assault carried the brown and white silks of the King Ranch flashing across the finish line, what a cheer went up on the Laureles! And a racing dynasty was born. The horse's speed and his utter refusal to let another horse beat him, carried him to a place in the record books with only ten other horses in history. As a three-year-old, he won the Kentucky Derby, the Preakness, and the Belmont. These three races constitute the ultimate in American racing—the Triple Crown.

The chestnut stallion won eight races in 1946 and four the next year. His total winnings were $672,500, a fabulous sum for that time. And he was not the only King Ranch horse running that year. Altogether in 1946 King Ranch horses won thirty-two races and well over a million dollars.

As with Monkey and Old Sorrel, something had made Bob Kleberg look at a limping colt and order his men to take care of him. But more than that. His instincts came to seem like magic. He could see a vision for the future and mold it to his hand. Because of its general manager, America came to look at King Ranch in a different way.

Assault, only one of ten horses to win the Triple Crown, is led to the winner's circle at the Kentucky Derby. His jockey wears the Running W on his silks.

Its luster was too bright to be burnished any more. With the big red horse's victories in 1946, the ranch that bred him moved into the realm of myth. Its owners would be perceived as movers and shakers, as titans of business, as Midases gifted with the golden touch, as lords of a private kingdom.

W W W

As with tradition dating back to the time of Robin Hood, the wild game on the lord's land belongs to the lord. As early as 1912, Caesar Kleberg had developed hunting rules that prevented wasteful shooting and the taking of game at watering holes or during times of drought. The wire fence that replaced the barbed wire was a mesh strung several inches above the ground so wild creatures might hop or crawl or slither underneath it.

Caesar was also responsible for establishing exotic nilgai antelope on the Texas coastal plain. The big beasts came from India and Pakistan where their range land is similar to that of Texas. Although they took twenty years to increase in sufficient numbers to be hunted, they now constitute an important attraction for hunters hoping for a thrilling shoot.

Because Caesar's rules had been more stringent than the poorly enforced rules of the State of Texas, in 1945 Bob Kleberg looked at his vast expanses and saw more deer, javelina, wild turkey, mourning dove, and quail than the rest of Texas put together.

The potential for wildlife to be a major auxiliary crop on South Texas range land did not escape his eye. With World War II over, American corporations were going overseas. King Ranch acreage could be leased to corporations for hunting trips for their employees and, more important, for their clients, particularly foreign clients, who had heard about the American cowboy from American movies.

Bob had always been an avid hunter. For his own pleasure and for the purpose of driving around friends and prospective customers, Bob ordered a customized Buick from General Motors. The hunting car, a monstrous white convertible with a straight-8 motor, was a grandson of the great touring cars of the first half of the twentieth century. The hood ornament bore the Running W brand. From grille to back bumper it gleamed with chrome and shouted luxury.

Metal and chrome triple rifle holsters were bolted to each fender, so the driver and the passenger beside him could pull the weapons out and pass them back. The front bumper had two small headlights, plus a massive chrome grille suitable for plowing through the brush in pursuit of whatever might take off running. Above the main headlights were two chrome stands, which could be fitted with seats, so really eager hunters could sit out in front of the driver and get a clear vision of everything that moved.

Bob and Dick's hunting car, the white Buick with custom grille, seat bases, and side holsters is proudly displayed in the King Ranch Museum. (Author photo)

The whole trunk space opened up into a dicky seat for more passengers or for packing with saddles and bridles to carry them to some distant hunting camp where the visitors could proceed on horseback farther into the *brasada*.

As the Buick roared past herds of sturdy red cattle, strong beautiful red horses, and pumping, pumping, pumping wells of black gold, the Klebergs must have felt like Kings of the World.

The King Ranch International

In 1944 Alice Gertrudis Kleberg died, the last of Richard King's children. She died as she had lived—on the ranch where she was born. Unlike her mother and father, her handiwork had been the raising of her children and grandchildren and the continuance of their legacy.

Two years later the last senior member of the household died also at the Santa Gertrudis. Caesar Kleberg, the bachelor and role model for the Kleberg sons and grandsons, was the last family member who could remember shaking hands with the Captain. His legacy was a foundation to promote wildlife management worldwide. King Ranch itself became a habitat laboratory where specialists could do their fieldwork.

Bob and Dick Kleberg assumed the joint leadership of the ranch and brought Dick's son Richard Jr. into the office. His schoolmates had been the sons of *Kineños*. They had taught him to rope and ride. He had learned their jokes, their games. They called him *Ricardito*, Little Ricky. From Corpus Christi, to Virginia Military Institute, to the University of Texas, he became a managerial assistant to Bob Kleberg to learn to run King Ranch from a desk chair, a pickup seat, and, of course, a saddle.

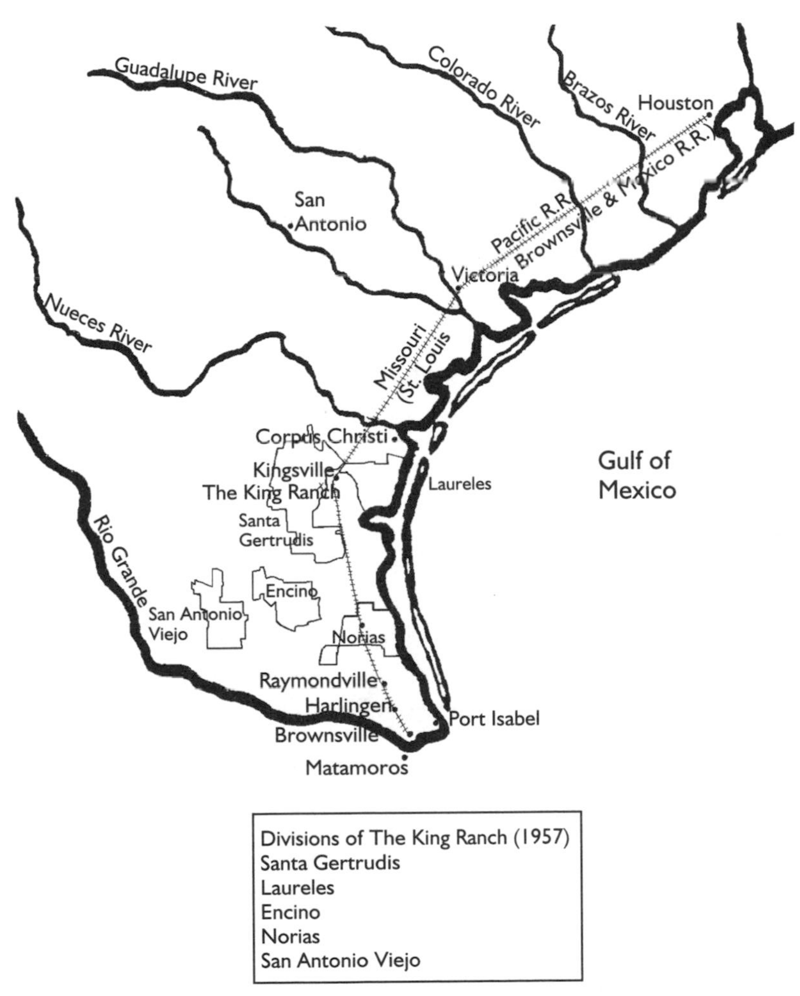

Of the three, Bob Kleberg quickly emerged as the visionary. In the tradition of his grandfather, he began to look beyond the million acres that made up their feudal kingdom. The railroad and the automobile were not the only means of transportation. Planes were flying across the oceans. The world was growing smaller. The King Ranch would be bigger than even Richard King could have possibly imagined.

If other American corporations could acquire properties overseas, the King Ranch could too.

First stop—the Gulf of Mexico. Bob Kleberg reasoned that Santa Gertrudis cattle had been sold to Cubans for twenty years. They had proved themselves superior to the Brahman and Criollo cattle that were the mainstays of the Cuban beef production.

Cuba in 1952 was a ranching paradise. The soil was fertile, the temperature and rainfall, ideal. Near the north central Camaguey Coast was a stretch of brush land and forest totally undeveloped. It was land nobody wanted. For the King Ranch it was ideal.

Forming a partnership with the Braga brothers, descendants of a Spanish colonial family, Bob Kleberg moved in bulls and heifers, stallions and mares, fencing and gates, and brush-clearing tractors. The result was King Ranch Cuba on forty thousand acres of land surrounded by sugarcane fields.

Initially a great deal of his purchase was covered with a thornbush called marabou. It covered the ground in an impenetrable mass that grew eight feet tall. Indeed twenty thousand acres of the partnership named Compañia Ganadera Becerra land was covered by it.

As he had done in South Texas with the mesquite, Bob made short work of the marabou. Though there were problems with the marshy soil, the growth rate of the cattle was two pounds a day. Start-up expenses had been high, but the venture looked to turn a handsome profit a few years down the road.

ꟽ ꟽ ꟽ

In 1953 King Ranch celebrated its centenary. Tom Lea, a respected Texas writer and artist, was commissioned to write its history and draw portraits of its heroes and heroines as well as its finest cattle and horses.

Winthrop Rockefeller and Richard M. Kleberg look over Santa Gertrudis cattle for sale at a breeders auction November 15, 1953. (From the Collections of the Texas/Dallas History and Archives Division, Dallas Public Library.)

One hundred years to the month after Richard King and Legs Lewis had ridden north from Brownsville, 150 guests, the top ranchers in Texas and around the world, were entertained at a conference at the King Ranch. The October conference was titled "Breeding Beef Cattle in Unfavorable Environments." Richard Mifflin Kleberg Sr., the Chairman of the Board, the polished politician, made the opening address.

A black tie occasion ended the conference where Robert Justus Kleberg Jr. made the closing address. The president and general manager of the ranch was always uneasy in the presence of so many sophisticated men including his polished brother. He read his speech in a monotone, but his words had the ring of sincerity when he invoked a dream and gave a call to arms.

The message of his speech was the duty of the American rancher as he saw it—to change grass into protein through beef production. Food, he maintained, had taken on a new dimension. Food was not only important to life and human progress, it was important in and to human affairs. Food was an instrument in diplomacy and a weapon of peace.

Bob Kleberg called for future expansion of beef production in wet and dry tropics and semidesert areas where the largest undeveloped regions of the world lay. He closed by saying, "the common-good effort...is man's struggle for freedom—for freedom from hunger, for freedom from oppression."

Bob Kleberg in the saddle.
(Courtesy of the Texas and Southwestern Cattle Raisers Foundation, Fort Worth, Texas.)

Afterwards he was relieved that he "got through it." Others at the banquet probably forgot it. But the speech was more than that. It was important for what it meant to him. At fifty-seven years of age, he set himself on a course that occupied his whole heart and mind for the twenty-one years he had left to live.

W W W

His first major disappointment came as King Ranch Cuba, his first foreign venture, fell to Fidel Castro. Just at the time when the Santa Gertrudis should have seen a big pay-off on their investment, the revolutionary leader came to power. The confiscation of the American capitalist ranch was high on his list. In the end Bob's three-million-dollar investment went down the drain.

To the end of his life Bob deeply resented the robbery. He aided Cuban refugees and helped the U.S. government in every way he could to bring relief to the persecuted there.

The stolen cattle were carted off to who knew where until an interesting tale was told the next year. In Russia, the Communist government invited Latin American business executives and educators to tour their country, so they might see for themselves the prosperity that had been achieved under the Communist system. On a ranch in the state of Georgia in the Soviet Union, the group was taken out to inspect a herd of dark cherry-red beef cattle. A Venezuelan executive came back to report to Bob that every one of those cows was branded with the Running W.

Thanks to his diversification, the loss of Cuba didn't dampen Bob's desire to take the ranch global. Embracing the newest technology, Bob persuaded Humble Oil to make a joint purchase of a DC-3. After the purchase of this first plane, he was never without air transportation. Eventually, he moved to a navigation computerized, Mach I, twin-engine jet certified to 42,000 feet and equipped to carry thirteen passengers and a crew of three. He excused the expense by estimating that it would extend his working life ten years.

In the air he headed for Venezuela where he set about creating a beef factory. The Mostrenco Ranch comprised 35,000 acres at the edge of the rain forest where rain fell three hundred days a year. The problems were different from any Bob had ever encountered. In this case the land had to be cleared, but at the same time it had to be protected. Land cleared of trees grows more trees at a fantastic rate unless the surface is immediately planted in grass. The tiniest root could be counted on to grow several inches a day. So wet and humid was the climate that fence posts actually began to grow. Barbed wire was strung between slender hardwood posts from a tree called *cola de ratón*. Within a few weeks, the posts took root. Two years later they were a living fence that never rotted.

The vista at Mostrenco was a broad expanse of lush grass disturbed at intervals by herds of cattle too short to be seen except by an occasional glimpse of a cherry-red head above the sea of green. Sometimes the only way to find the herd was to stand on a tower and train binoculars on moving grass.

The initial estimate was that Mostrenco could produce four thousand cattle yearly. The truth was soon seen. The grass grew to be eight feet tall so fast that even that number of cattle couldn't eat enough of it to keep it low. Skinny cattle actually had to be smuggled in from nearby Columbia to keep it eaten down. In one year nineteen thousand head of cattle were fattened, and still the managers couldn't keep up with the grass growth.

El Cedral, another huge property in Venezuela close to the Amazon basin, was purchased as King Ranch cattle grew and prospered. Problems with foot rot on the damp ground and hoof-and-mouth disease, the scourge of South America, were attacked with the same enthusiasm and certitude that had done away with cattle ticks and phosphorus deficiency. Even the problems posed by alligators and piranhas didn't dampen Bob's spirits.

At its peak of production, King Ranch Venezuela was by many estimates "the most beautiful ranch" in the world.

King Ranch Brazil presented different problems. There Bob went into partnership with International Packers, a subsidiary of Swift and Company. Five ranches were combined to total 147,000 acres. It had fifty inches of rainfall annually that nourished a red soil, high in iron and minerals. The land was perfect for Santa Gertrudis cattle.

Unfortunately, the manager would not do what Bob told him to do. He ignored direct orders that the land was to be nurtured and protected even at the expense of putting weight on the cattle. When Bob returned he saw that the land had been purposefully overgrazed. The magnificent stand of grass that he'd purchased had been reduced to stubble so the manager could turn a quick profit.

Bob Kleberg was furious, but the damage had been done. Instead of grass, the land was covered with weeds and brush. One of the King Ranch CEO's paramount occupations was with grass. As he expanded his holdings, he was constantly on the lookout for new varieties. These he brought home to the Santa Gertrudis to experiment with. Seething at the sight of pastures that had virtually been put out of production, he demoted the ranch manager on the spot.

ᴡ ᴡ ᴡ

While he was buying worldwide, he didn't neglect the United States. Just south of Lake Okeechobee in Florida, he bought 40,000 acres of muck land which he named the Big

B. The ranch was a disappointment. The land was so soggy that trees wouldn't grow. The tallest things in the pasture were the cattle. Ironically, today the Big B is a St. Augustine grass sod farm that produces sixteen million dollars annually, much more than the cattle do on the present ranch in South Texas.

Bob bought the Buck and Doe Ranch in Pennsylvania as a feed lot for eastern beef markets. He bought King Ranch Kentucky for his Thoroughbreds. Like his grandfather before him, if he saw an opportunity, he took advantage of it. He might have had the ghost of Richard King standing at his shoulder to whisper in his ear, "Buy land and never sell."

ꟿ ꟿ ꟿ

Bob took King Ranch to the Argentine, which he regarded as the "best damn cattle country in the world." The acquisition of these four properties in ideal cattle country was odd in the light of Bob's stated purpose to take cattle into areas where they had been only marginally successful. Furthermore, the political climate created by the dictator Juan Perón and his wife Evita was so unstable that Bob had to delay bringing his organization into the country.

The cattle ranchers of Argentina made a good target for the Peróns, who were intent on annihilating them to draw attention from the real problems of poverty and lack of equality within the country. For these reasons Bob kept his acquisitions unpublicized until he was ready to make his move in 1967.

When the Peróns were overthrown, Bob moved in with his Santa Gertrudis stock. For the first time the world was invited to watch as the All-American breed stood head to head against the best British Shorthorns and Herefords and Scots Aberdeen Angus the Argentinians had been importing for years. The contest was one of grazing and multiplying in temperate climates on the *estancieros* with their incomparable alfalfa pastures.

Bob was throwing down the gauntlet to the world. The King Ranch did well, even though the ranch managers behaved very much like the manager in Brazil. Hide-bound by tradition, they would not obey Bob's orders that would have raised production. He was never able to prove the superiority of the Santa Gertrudis over the other breeds. When the unthinkable happened and Juan Perón was returned to power, the ranch created more problems than it solved.

ꟺ ꟺ ꟺ

At the insistence of Australian Dr. R. B. Kelley, head of the Division of Animal Health and Production, Commonwealth Science and Industrial Research Organization, Bob took King Ranch to Australia. Dr. Kelley had bought a Santa Gertrudis bull for a herd in Queensland where the animal had proved exceptionally adaptable.

It is often said that Australians and Americans are closer kin than Australians and English. If that is so, then they must be closer to Texans than to anyone else in the world. Bob loved the Australians, who were just like Texans, he maintained, with funny accents.

However, he was hesitant about starting the operation there because he knew he wouldn't be able to have a hand in managing it. The distance between King Ranch, Kingsville, and King Ranch, Queensland was too great.

ꟺ ꟺ ꟺ

Another problem of a graver nature was facing him at home. He had handpicked his successor in 1940 when his brother's son, Richard M. Kleberg Jr., graduated from the University of Texas. *Ricardito* had been the logical choice.

He was a great-grandson of Richard King. He could carry the family into the twenty-first century.

Unfortunately, *Ricardito's* health had begun to fail. He did not have the overpowering drive to make King Ranch more and more and more. For twenty years he had not worked well in the shade of his handsome, recondite father and his brilliant, dedicated uncle.

Over seventy years old, Bob Kleberg faced the grim future with no one to replace him. Still he did not stop. A man with a mission, he carried his plans forward.

Before venturing into Australia, he took care to find men who could assume the responsibilities that Mifflin Kenedy had assumed in the schemes of Richard King. He took on three very capable partners. Sir Rupert Clarke, baronet, was a pastoralist and investment banker. Peter Baillieu was a trained property manager. Sam Hordern was one of Australia's leading businessmen-agriculturalists.

The man who put the mix together was W. S. Robinson, Australia's premier businessman, entrepreneur, and intimate of Winston Churchill. In 1960 King Ranch Australia opened six ranches, or stations, with four hundred head of "Santas" as the Australians called the big cherry-red cattle. (They couldn't get their tongues around the word Gertrudis.) Just after the cattle arrived, ten of the young imported bulls were auctioned for an average of $2,595 a head, a record for Australian cattle at that time.

So proud was Bob of this ranch that on his last trip to Queensland, he took along his friend Tom Lea, who wrote a book and illustrated it as he had *The King Ranch* a quarter century before. *In the Crucible of the Sun* was printed privately and copies presented to the libraries of all the land grant colleges and universities in the United States.

ꟽ ꟽ ꟽ

In his seventies, Bob took the King Ranch to Spain and to Morocco. He made a trip to Africa and fell in love with the fierce Kalahari Desert, one of the dryest places on earth. He believed it had great potential. He was one of the first men to recognize that man is not a good steward of the land. Indeed, wherever man goes, he creates deserts. In an effort to educate his peers, Bob used the King Ranch as a great tool and example of how ranching should be. Rather than make deserts, Bob Kleberg wanted to reclaim them all.

To stand behind him and look past his hat was to see land nobody wanted. To know his thinking was to share in his vision of a worldwide sea of grass.

In October 1974, as Bob lay dying in St. Luke's Hospital at the Baylor Medical Center in Houston, Lea was able to place the first copy of *In the Crucible of the Sun* in his friend's hands.

The process by which King Ranch Texas had grown—by careful breeding, by protecting the cattle from parasites, by digging water wells to take them through the droughts, by husbanding the grass—made King Ranch Australia Bob Kleberg's most successful achievement.

ꟿ ꟿ ꟿ

Bob took King Ranch everywhere despite the problems. He lived with the premise that in a business of the scope that he had cut for himself, about twenty percent of it would be in trouble at any one time. More problematical was the fact that it wouldn't always be the same twenty percent. Put a brush fire out in one spot and a lightning strike will start another one somewhere else. In the end he had no more life to give to the fight.

Robert Justus Kleberg Jr. died on October 13, 1974, at the age of seventy-eight. Cancer had felled him as it had his grandfather, although he had lived many more years than the Captain.

When his uncle died, Richard M. Kleberg Jr., Ricardito, was too ill from emphysema to take his place.

Unfortunately, the next fifteen years were not so kind to Bob's memory and his achievements as those years had been to the founder of King Ranch Texas.

He would have hated the gusto with which King Ranch International was sold at a great profit after his death.

Meanwhile Back at the Ranch—

When Bob died his two nephews Bobby Shelton and B. K. Johnson came forward to make presentations to the board of directors. They were the sons of his baby sister Sarah Spohn, whom he had all but reared. Each asked to take over the ranch. Each was refused. The comment from one of the board of directors was, "One dictator in this family is enough."

Both the men walked away leaving King Ranch to be run by committee rather than by a strong man with a vision. Jim Clement, an East Coast-trained businessman, one of Bob's brothers-in-law, headed the board.

The approximately sixty stockholders decided they should get a larger share of the King Ranch profits—seventy-five percent annually. Only twenty-five percent was left to run the ranch and continue development. The Thoroughbred horses and overseas ranches that did not show a big profit were put on the auction block. The proceeds from the sales also went almost entirely to the stockholders.

Furthermore, the majority of the stockholders had no real interest in the ranch other than the fact that it had made them millionaires overnight. They were venture capitalists, doctors, lawyers, professors.

At the King Ranch today. Beside the visitors center is the ranch business office. (Author photo)

Many members of the older generation were worried about what this extraction of capital would do to the ranch. Their worry was completely justified. They feared the same fate as so many of America's great family fortunes. If the younger generation is content to live off the income rather than use it to improve and maintain the ranch, then the ranch will very shortly cease to exist. One among them must be found to manage the ranch.

In 1977 Stephen Justus Kleberg, the son of Richard M. Kleberg Jr., came back to the ranch to take over the cattle raising opcration. The *Kineños* nicknamed him "Tio" because he resembled his great uncle, the fabled Bob Kleberg.

He has always looked to make the King Ranch better. Since the oil royalties have decreased, he has come to the conclusion that resource management is a better plan for the ranch than strictly cattle. He has begun to farm cotton and milo. He has leased more than half the land for commercial hunting operations.

Most impressive was his development of Santa Cruz cattle. The new cattle are a composite breed, dedicated to providing "designer" beef to cater to America's interest in ever leaner meat. The Santa Cruz, whose name means "cross," are one-half Santa Gertrudis, one-quarter Red Angus, and one-quarter Gelbvieh, a German breed.

They are leaner and very fertile. They reach sexual maturity in just over a year, and one cow can produce thirteen calves in a lifetime as opposed to the Santa Gertrudis cow that produces twelve. They still have the red color of the Santa Gertrudis, although the shade is honey red. So the red cattle that Alice King Kleberg liked so much still graze in the green fields.

The new red Santa Cruz cattle—more fertile, faster growing, leaner "designer" beef for health-conscious Americans. (Author photo)

Tio is just like his father and his great-uncle, a servant of the land. He and his wife, Janell, live on the ranch and answer their own phone, listed in the Kingsville telephone directory. Tio feels strongly the obligation that the King family has to the *Kineños*, whom he regards with the same affection and respect that tradition demands.

He allocates $150,000 a year for Kingsville civic projects. He and Janell participate in the duties of the town. He oversees the King Ranch Saddle Shop and the King Ranch-owned hardware store in town.

When in the eighties the board of directors decided that the ranch could no longer support seven hundred *Kineños*, he had to look them in the eye and tell them that they no longer had jobs, nor did their children in the future.

His strength of character and his hot temper, perhaps inherited from Richard King, have made him an ideal leader but a difficult man to deal with. He has never been a corporate player.

Although he has been the only one willing to run the ranch, the stockholders have not always been pleased with his decisions and especially with his expenditures. Perhaps the very nature of the King heritage is that many of his descendants are strong-willed with strong opinions.

The two CEOs who took charge, one after another, after Bob Kleberg's death, began to take steps in different directions. To its acreages were added a citrus grove and a sod farm in Florida, an alfalfa farm in Arizona, and oil and gas wells in the Gulf of Mexico. Moreover, the cotton and milo farms brought in more than the cattle.

The revenues rose and the stockholders were eager for more. The cattle industry made less money than these new projects. The stockholders wanted to lock in their profits.

So the hunt began for an outside chief executive—one who was not a family member. The committee set out to find its third CEO. Jack Hunt was the head of the publicly held Tejon Ranch Company in California, a 270,000-acre operation that involved commercial real estate, farming, recreation, mineral extraction, and ranching (only a small part was ranching).

Hunt is the embodiment of the modern CEO, with his eye on ways to make money and increase profits. In 1997 the pre-tax profits of the King Ranch were more than $32 million. The company had a whopping $200 million in the bank or invested in securities. It had almost no debt. The new drilling technology had found deeper oil pools on King Ranch land. The approximately eighty family members divided $36 million in dividends from the corporation. Nobody had anything to complain about.

Jack Hunt had no reason to keep Tio Kleberg, who had often crossed swords with him. The ranch was a small part of the operation. A figurehead of a Kleberg would work just as well as a working man.

So with the consent of the board of directors, Jack Hunt called Tio to Houston and discharged him as general manager. At the same time the great-great grandson of Richard King was promoted to a seat on the board of directors. Effective June 1, 1998, after twenty-eight years, the last Kleberg no longer had the responsibility for the stewardship of the land.

ꟿ ꟿ ꟿ

What happens to the King Ranch now lies in the hands of a group of leaders, most of whom set foot on the ranch itself only for the annual stockholders meeting. Since only the family can own stock, the family will continue to own the ranch at least in theory. Unfortunately, the painting of the mesquite tree in the library may mean nothing to the twigs out on its uppermost branches far, far removed from its roots.

Will they grow so far away from the ranch that they come to regard it as a relic of a bygone era fit only for the auction block? Will they continue to draw strength from it as a touchstone of where they have come from and where they are going?

As a century and a half of greatness draws to a close, the future of King Ranch as with the future of Texas may very well belong not to rugged individuals who can move cattle, but to hard-headed individuals who move money.

Glossary

of Spanish terms not immediately defined in the text.

arroyo(s)—A narrow gully with steep dirt walls and a flat floor that is a creek or rivulet when it's wet, but it's usually dry. Arroyos are bad places to camp because of flash floods.

Boca del Rio—Mouth of the River; in this case the mouth of the Rio Grande.

bravo—A brave man, one who shows off for the ladies or for his peers in reckless ways. Also refers to *Rio Bravo*, the Mexican name for the Rio Grande.

brasada(s)—The brush country of South Texas. Any country so overgrown with cactus and thorn trees that it is virtually impenetrable to a man on horseback.

Brazos de Santiago—Arms of Saint James as in *El Paso de los Brazos de Santiago*. The south tip of land that forms the southern passage into Laguna Madre due east of Port Isabel in South Texas.

burro—A little donkey, usually gray although some have a cross marked in black on their backs at the shoulders.

caporál(es)—Foreman or assistant foreman. The use of the Spanish word indicates that he is a Mexican. He manages or bosses a sheep or cattle ranch.

carreta(s)—Two-wheeled Mexican oxcart. Its wheels were solid pieces of wood or two solid half-circles joined together at the hub.

casa(s)—A house.

cola de ratón—Literally tail of rat. A type of tree that grows in South America.

colonia—Villages or groupings of huts where people from Mexico might live together on a Texas prairie. Usually the huts are constructed out of scrap lumber or other handy materials.

concho(s)—Shell. Also the disk-shaped silver ornaments that decorate all manner of leather goods. The Navajos are particularly famous for making and wearing them.

El Sal Viejo—Old Salt. A mostly dry lake in deep South Texas where salt has been mined for centuries.

entrada—An entry, sometimes with formal or religious significance. In this case the pilgrimage on which King led his new people, the *Kineños*, across the Rio Grande into South Texas.

gente—People. The word infers that the people are good and reasonable. Civilized.

gringos and greasers—Derogatory terms for Anglos (gringos) and Mexicans (greasers) used by both groups to insult each other.

gritas—Hooting, shouting, making a great noise. Sometimes rousing songs will finish with shrill *gritas*.

jacál(es)—A mud hut usually constructed of whatever trees and brush are at hand, then plastered over with mud. *Jacales* have dirt floors and no amenities.

junta—A meeting or conference, usually referring to a meeting to plan strategy for some important business deal or piece of government legislation. A *junta* is often associated with a revolution.

Juaristas—Followers of Benito Juárez.

Laguna Madre—Mother Lagoon. The long bay of shallow water that separates Padre (Father) Island from the mainland of Texas from Brazos de Santiago to Corpus Christi.

los diablos Tejanos—The Texan devils.

monte—Pasture, grass. Although the word ordinarily means mountain or mount, in Central America and Mexico it may refer to thicket, pasture, or grass.

ranchero(s)—A ranch owner.

rancho(ito)—A ranch or with the suffix a little ranch.

resaca(s)—A brackish finger of the Gulf of Mexico. It may also mean the mud and slime left by a flood when a hurricane blows in.

riata(s)—Also reata. A cowboy's rope of braided leather. Usually a very long rope, sometimes as much as forty to sixty feet. Some *vaqueros* could make catches from fifty feet away.

rincón—As in *Rincón de Santa Gertrudis*, meaning hidden valley, a protected spot, a good place for a house.

Rurales—The Mexican equivalent of the Arizona Rangers—a paramilitary force that operated in rural areas. They operated as a group rather than individually as Texas Rangers did. During the Mexican Revolution the corps consisted of killers and bandits released from prison for the purpose of terrorizing the countryside.

vaquero—A Mexican cowman who did all the chores required to maintain a herd of cows. Not to be used interchangeably with *caballeros,* since the word horseman usually referred to one of higher rank, even a nobleman.

Bibliography

Blevins, Winfred. *Dictionary of the American West*. New York: Facts on File, Inc., 1993.

Botkin, B. A., ed. *A Treasury of Western Folklore*. New York: Crown Publishers, Inc., 1951.

Clayton, Lawrence. *Historic Ranches of Texas*. Austin: University of Texas Press, 1993.

Cypher, John. *Bob Kleberg and the King Ranch, A Worldwide Sea of Grass*. Austin: University of Texas Press, Austin, 1995.

Durham, George. *Taming the Nueces Strip, The Story of McNelly's Rangers*. Austin: University of Texas Press, 1962.

Edwards, Elwin Hartley. *The Ultimate Horse Book*. New York: Dorling Kindersley, Inc., 1991.

Estes, Clarissa Pinkola. *Women Who Run with the Wolves*. New York: Ballantine, 1992.

Fehrenbach, T. R. *Lone Star, A History of Texas and the Texans*. New York: The Macmillan Company, 1968.

Hollandsworth, Skip, "When We Were Kings," *Texas Monthly*, August 1988, pp. 112-117, 140-144.

Horswell, Cindy, "Longhorn Breed Boasts Storied Past," *The Dallas Morning News*, December 8, 1996, p. 52A.

"King Ranch Introduces King Ranch Santa Cruz," Kingsville, Texas, King Ranch Inc., n. d.

Kleberg Jr., Robert J., "A Review of the Development of the Breed, Historical Data About the Origin of the Santa Gertrudis Breed," n. d.

Lea, Tom. *The King Ranch. Vol. I & II*. Boston: Little, Brown, and Company, 1957.

Monday, Jane Clements and Betty Bailey Colley. *Voices from the Wild Horse Desert, The Vaquero Families of the King and Kenedy Ranches*. Austin: University of Texas Press, 1997.

Rhoad, A. O. and R. J. Kleberg Jr., "The Development of a Superior Family in the Modern Quarter Horse," *The Journal of Heredity*, Washington, D.C., August 1947, 37:8, p. 226-238.

Tanner, Ogden. *The Ranchers*. Alexandria, Virginia: Time-Life Books, 1977.

Tash, Lowell H. and J. M. Jones. "Phosphorus: Experiments Show This Mineral Essential to Greater Beef Production in South Texas," *The Cattleman*, February 1947.

Wyman, Walker D. *The Wild Horse of the West*. Lincoln: University of Nebraska Press, 1945.

Index